Animal Farm

George Orwell

A GCSE revision guide
devised and written by Janet Oliver

The right of Janet Oliver to be identified as Author of this Work has been asserted by her in accordance with the Copyright, Designs and Patents Act 1988

First published 2018

ISBN 978-1-9998402-8-0

© Vega Publishing LTD 2018

All rights reserved. No part of this publication may be reproduced, stored in a retrieval system, or transmitted in any form or by any means, electronic, mechanical, photocopying, recording, or otherwise, without the prior written permission of the Publisher.

Restricted copying in the United Kingdom issued by the Copyright Licensing Agency Ltd, Saffron House, 6-10 Kirby Street, London EC1N 8TS

Animal Farm by George Orwell (© George Orwell, 1945). Reproduced by kind permission of Bill Hamilton as Literary Executor of the Estate of the Late Sonia Brownell and Secker & Warburg Ltd.

Vega Publishing LTD, 12 Glebe Avenue, Woodford Green, Essex IG8 9HB United Kingdom

Design by Martin Cadwallader

Contents

	Introduction - how to use this book	4
	Timeline - plot summary	6
Section 1	**Napoleon** - character analysis	8
Section 2	**Snowball** - character analysis	14
Section 3	**Boxer & Clover** - character analysis	20
Section 4	**Squealer & Propaganda** - character analysis	26
Section 5	**Old Major** - character analysis	32
Section 6	**The Minor Characters** - exploration of the text	38
Section 7	**Education** - exploration of a theme	44
Section 8	**Power & Corruption** - exploration of a theme	50
Section 9	**Hopes & Dreams** - exploration of a theme	56
Section 10	**Setting** - exploration of the text	62
Section 11	**Genre & Narrative** - exploration of the text	68
Section 12	**Failure of the Revolution** - exploration of a theme	74
Section 13	**Quotations** - recap and revise	80
Section 14	**Glossary** - explanation of terms	83

Introduction
How to use this book

'Animal Farm' is one of Orwell's most famous novels. The story of the oppressed animals who overthrow their masters only to end up in an even worse state of servitude has entertained millions of readers for over fifty years. Its universal appeal is obvious but tackling such a wide-ranging story in a short exam is a real challenge.

This guide is written and laid out to help you with your revision of 'Animal Farm' and to ensure that your examination response is focused and clear. It is designed to show you how to address the most important elements that the examiner is looking for:

- **Language analysis**
- **Effective use of quotations**
- **Exploration of themes**
- **Understanding of character**
- **Orwell's intentions and messages**

The book is divided into sections of characters and themes with a box at the top of each section which gives a strong, clear overview of the character or theme.

The section is then dealt with using 5-8 key quotations which are in **bold** font. Literary devices are in **bold italics**.

The analysis of each quotation relates directly to the theme or character. Some of the points are fairly straightforward and some are much more analytical.

The **context** is added at the end to show how it can be woven into an answer with a relevant quotation. Context means the social, historical and literary influences of the time that Orwell was writing in and how these are reflected in the novel.

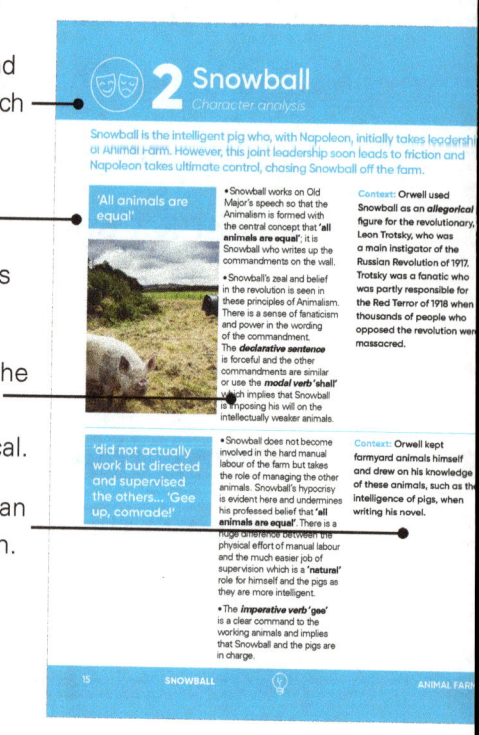

There is also a yellow box entitled 'Grade 9 Exploration' in each chapter. This shows you how you can look at alternative interpretations of the novel, which are crucial for gaining a grade of 7 or above.

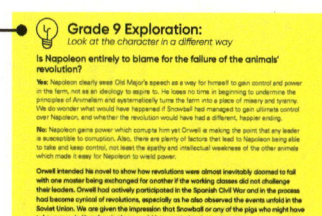

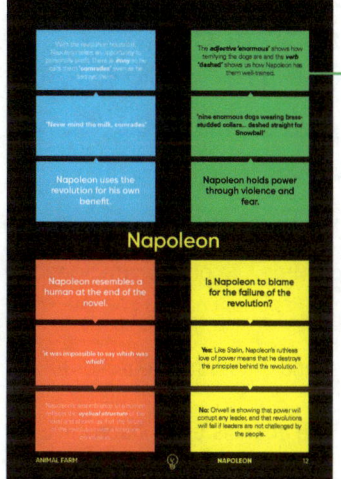

Look out for the colourful mindmap. It condenses four main points from the chapter, including the Grade 9 Exploration box, into four strands. The information is in a shortened format; if you want to keep your revision really focused, use the mind map to make sure you remember the key features of the chapter.

The sample essay follows. This is based on a 4 paragraph formula which answers the question clearly and analytically. The font is small as there is so much detail but, if you are wondering what a top level answer looks like, do read it carefully.

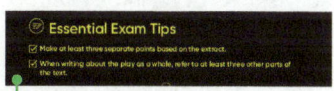

Below that there is a box with essential exam tips: lots of good ideas and reminders that will help you on exam day.

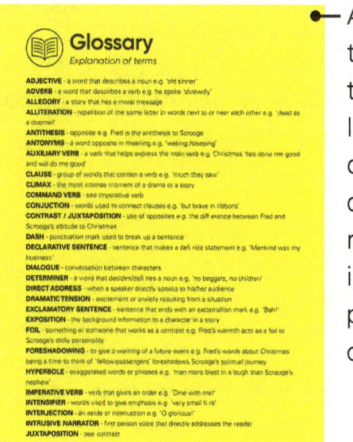

At the back of the book, there is a glossary of all the literary terms and a list of the quotations with chapter references. You really don't need to learn these references; they are only included to help you find the place in the novel for your own revision.

ANIMAL FARM — **INTRODUCTION** — **5**

Timeline
Plot Summary

The story of 'Animal Farm' follows a cyclical structure as the animals rebel against their human master but soon find themselves once again ruled by a different tyrant. The story follows the events of the Russian revolution in the early twentieth century; key events are indicated in the bold context boxes.

Chapter 1
- Old Major calls a meeting to tell the animals about his dream. First, he outlines in a passionate speech all that is wrong with the animals' lives. He blames humans for abusing the animals and taking the products of their hard work.
- He encourages the animals to rebel and overthrow their human masters, and sets out a series of rules or advice about how to organise society after the rebellion.
- He ends with recounting his dream of a wonderful England where all of the animals enjoy happy lives of freedom.

Karl Marx was the founder of communism. His ideas were used by Lenin and other communists to inspire the Russian workers to riot against their rulers.

Chapter 2
- Even though Major dies soon after, his words have inspired the animals to become active in preparing for a rebellion. The pigs take the lead in organising the other animals, and turn Major's words into a school of thought called Animalism.
- Mr Jones is so drunk that he forgets to feed the animals. Hungry and angry, the animals launch an attack against their masters and chase Jones and the other humans off the farm.
- The animals are now in charge of themselves and the farm. They agree to keep Jones' farmhouse as a museum.
- The pigs tell the animals that they have learnt to read and have condensed Major's advice into seven commandments which they write on the barn's wall.
- The pigs milk the cows. Later, the animals find out that the milk has disappeared.

In 1917, the Russian people rioted against their ruler Tsar Nicholas II. The Tsar abdicated and the people, led by the Bolsheviks, took charge of Russia.

Chapter 3
- The animals successfully bring in the harvest.
- Weekly meetings are set up at which the pigs take a lead. Napoleon and Snowball are constantly at odds with one another.
- Snowball organises many committees to improve the animals' lives. The reading and writing classes are most successful.
- Napoleon takes the puppies in order to educate them. It is discovered that the milk has been taken by the pigs. The pigs then take the apples for themselves.

Chapter 4
- Animal Farm becomes famous throughout the country, and animals in other farms show signs of rebellion against their masters.
- The humans feel under threat and help Jones attack the farm.

- Snowball leads the animals in driving the humans off the farm in what becomes known as the Battle of the Cowshed.

Between 1917 and 1922, armies loyal to the Tsar tried to take back control of Russia.

Chapter 5
- Mollie leaves the farm to live with humans.
- Divisions deepen between Snowball and Napoleon, especially over the plans for the windmill.
- At a meeting, Napoleon sets his dogs on Snowball. Snowball is chased off the farm.
- Work starts on the windmill.

In 1928, Stalin forced Trotsky to leave the Soviet Union.

Chapter 6
- Work continues slowly on the windmill.
- Napoleon announces the decision to trade with the local farmers. The pigs move into the farmhouse.
- The windmill falls down in a storm. Snowball is blamed for this.

Stalin moved Russia away from an agrarian (farming) society to an industrialised one.

Chapter 7
- Conditions on the farm are hard.
- The hens refuse to give their eggs to be sold at market but Napoleon starves them until they agree.

Stalin forced the farms in the Soviet Union to come under state control and hand over their crops, materials and animal produce. The peasants opposed this.

- Snowball is accused of vandalising the farm.
- There is a meeting at which various animals confess to being in partnership with Snowball and of committing different crimes. They are executed by the dogs.

Between 1936-1938, Stalin used Trotsky as a scapegoat, with show trials and executions of those accused of being in league with him.

Chapter 8
- The animals work ever harder.
- Napoleon creates a 'cult of personality' which means the animals are expected to idolise him.

Stalin created a cult of personality which encouraged the Russian people to worship him.

- Napoleon strikes a deal with the farmer Mr Frederick to sell him timber. However, the bank notes that Frederick uses are fakes.
- Frederick and his men attack the farm and destroy the windmill. They are fought off but the animals have many casualties.

Stalin negotiated a treaty with Germany which Hitler betrayed when he invaded the Soviet Union in 1941.

- Napoleon and the pigs start to drink alcohol.

Chapter 9
- Life on the farm becomes ever harder.
- Boxer grows old and weak. He is taken away by the horse slaughterer to be killed.

Chapter 10
- Years pass.
- The windmill is built but the animals do not see any of the benefits that they were promised.
- Napoleon stands on two trotters and carries a whip.
- The humans visit the pigs but the friendly atmosphere soon becomes aggressive.
- They seem to be bonding but then there is an argument over cheating at cards.

Stalin became allies with Britain and the United States but this alliance fell apart with the start of the Cold War.

1 Napoleon
Character analysis

Napoleon is the power-hungry pig who takes control of the farm. Under his leadership, the principles of Animalism are ignored until, by the end, Napoleon is more human than pig and holds complete power over the other animals.

'Napoleon... large, rather fierce-looking Berkshire boar'

- Orwell deliberately chose the name 'Napoleon' to give the reader a clue about the pig's power-loving personality, using the name of the French emperor who overthrew the government in the name of the people but who ended up a military tyrant.

- The **adjectives** **'large'** and **'fierce-looking'** give Napoleon a sense of formidable strength.

Context: Napoleon is the allegorical figure for Joseph Stalin, the strong, brutal dictator of the Soviet Union.

'Never mind the milk, comrades,' cried Napoleon, placing himself in front of the buckets'

- Napoleon takes the first opportunity to personally profit from the revolution by taking control of the fresh milk which is later mixed into the pigs' mash. Even with the revolution only hours old, Napoleon's self-interest is evident. Orwell meant this incident to be a turning point in the story, showing through the novel's **structure** how the revolution is doomed from the beginning because of the ruthlessness of characters such as Napoleon.

- There is **irony** in the way that Napoleon addresses the other animals with the title **'comrades'** which implies solidarity even as he plans to betray them.

- We are given a sense of his physical presence by the way he puts his body **'in front of the buckets'**. There is a sense of physical threat in his action, **foreshadowing** how he will use violence and intimidation later on in the novel.

Quote	Analysis	Context
'nine enormous dogs wearing brass-studded collars... dashed straight for Snowball'	• Napoleon uses the dogs as a way controlling the animals. Here, he uses them to get rid of his rival, Snowball. • The **adjectives** **'enormous'** and **'brass-studded'** in the description help create a sense of violent brutality while the **verb** **'dashed'** shows their speed. Napoleon has the dogs well-trained in his service and uses them ruthlessly throughout the novel to control the animals through fear and intimidation.	**Context:** Snowball represents Trotsky, Stalin's rival in the newly-formed Soviet Union. Napoleon's vicious eviction of Snowball reflects the way he deals with rivals- with contempt and ruthlessness. Stalin used a brutal secret police to control the Soviet Union; the dogs represent this police squad, the NKVD.
'Napoleon is always right'	• Boxer's words show how Napoleon is revered by the workers. • It also shows how Napoleon allows no room for dissent, the **adverb** **'always'** reflecting how absolute Napoleon's power is. Arguably, Boxer's faith in his leader indicates how charismatic Napoleon is, inspiring great devotion. Certainly, this devotion keeps the animals passive.	
'Smiling beatifically, and wearing both his decorations, Napoleon reposed... with the money at his side' 	• Napoleon triumphantly displays the money he has received in payment for the timber. • This victory celebration which he takes part in shows not just his love of power, it also shows a cunning understanding of how power works. Napoleon is creating a cult of personality which means that he is constructing a public image of himself as omniscient (all-knowing) and omnipotent (all-powerful). • Orwell uses **satire** in the image of Napoleon **'smiling beatifically'**; the **adverb** **'beatifically'** means saint-like but Napoleon is behaving in the exact opposite way, signalling to us that Orwell is making Napoleon a figure of fun. This is reinforced later when we find out that the bank notes are fakes.	**Context:** Stalin created a cult of personality that helped him maintain power through creating an image of himself as god-like.

'No animal shall drink alcohol to excess'	• Napoleon uses Squealer with his skill at twisting the truth to help control the animals, and here Squealer alters the fifth commandment to reflect the pigs' new habit of drinking alcohol.	**Context: Stalin used written propaganda to control the population through the government-controlled newspaper Pravda.**
	• Napoleon and Squealer wield power through deceit and manipulation. Their literacy and the other animals' lack of education means that it is easy for Napoleon to exploit his power.	• The commandments are changed throughout the story, reflecting how Napoleon consistently erodes the principles of Animalism.
'it was impossible to say which was which'	• At the end of the novel, Napoleon is walking on two legs, sleeping in a bed and is, essentially, a human; so much so that the watching animals cannot tell Napoleon and Mr Pilkington apart.	
	• Napoleon's transformation reflects the **cyclical structure** of the novel and shows us that the failure of the revolution was a foregone conclusion.	

Grade 9 Exploration:
Look at the character in a different way

Is Napoleon entirely to blame for the failure of the animals' revolution?

Yes: Napoleon clearly sees Old Major's speech as a way for himself to gain control and power in the farm, not as an ideology to aspire to. He loses no time in beginning to undermine the principles of Animalism and systematically turns the farm into a place of misery and tyranny. We do wonder what would have happened if Snowball had managed to gain ultimate control over Napoleon, and whether the revolution would have had a different, happier ending.

No: Napoleon gains power which corrupts him yet Orwell is making the point that any leader is susceptible to corruption. Also, there are plenty of factors that lead to Napoleon being able to take and keep control, not least the apathy and intellectual weakness of the other animals which made it easy for Napoleon to wield power.

Orwell intended his novel to show how revolutions were almost inevitably doomed to fail with one master being exchanged for another if the working classes did not challenge their leaders. Orwell had actively participated in the Spanish Civil War and in the process had become cynical of revolutions, especially as he also observed the events unfold in the Soviet Union. We are given the impression that Snowball or any of the pigs who might have taken power in Napoleon's place would have ended up just as corrupt.

Napoleon

With the revolution hours old, Napoleon takes an opportunity to personally profit. There is *irony* as he calls them **'comrades'** even as he betrays them.

'Never mind the milk, comrades'

Napoleon uses the revolution for his own benefit.

The *adjective* **'enormous'** shows how terrifying the dogs are and the *verb* **'dashed'** shows us how Napoleon has them well-trained.

'nine enormous dogs wearing brass-studded collars... dashed straight for Snowball'

Napoleon holds power through violence and fear.

Napoleon resembles a human at the end of the novel.

'it was impossible to say which was which'

Napoleon's resemblance to a human reflects the **cyclical structure** of the novel and shows us that the failure of the revolution was a foregone conclusion.

Is Napoleon to blame for the failure of the revolution?

Yes: Like Stalin, Napoleon's ruthless love of power means that he destroys the principles behind the revolution.

No: Orwell is showing that power will corrupt any leader, and that revolutions will fail if leaders are not challenged by the people.

Sample GCSE Exam Question & Answer

Q: How does Orwell use the character of Napoleon to show ideas about power?

✓ Start with the point that Napoleon is a character who enjoys power

Napoleon is the power-hungry pig who takes control of Animal Farm. Under his leadership, the principles of Animalism are deliberately ignored until, by the end, Napoleon is more human than pig and is in complete control of the other animals on the farm. Orwell deliberately chose the name Napoleon to give the reader a clue about his power-loving personality, using the name of the French emperor who overthrew the government in the name of the people but ended up a tyrant. Orwell uses Napoleon as the ***allegorical*** figure of Joseph Stalin, the ruthless, brutal dictator of the Soviet Union and, even in the opening physical description of Napoleon, we are given a sense of formidable strength in the ***adjectives*** **'large'** and **'rather fierce-looking'**. Napoleon clearly enjoys wielding power and this is seen when Napoleon triumphantly displays the money he has received in payment for the timber: **'smiling beatifically, and wearing both his decorations, Napoleon reposed... with the money at his side'**. He is essentially greedy and ostentatious (a show-off) as he actually lies amongst the piles of notes yet this victory celebration which he takes part in shows not just his love of power and desire to lord it over the other animals, it also shows a cunning understanding of how power works. Napoleon is creating a cult of personality which means that he is constructing a public image of himself as omniscient (all-knowing) and omnipotent (all-powerful). By flaunting himself, Napoleon ensures that the other animals visibly see him as superior and also, as participants, they are passively accepting his position of authority. This is a technique used by dictators throughout history and certainly used by Stalin who Napoleon represents in the novel. Orwell uses ***satire*** in the ***image*** of Napoleon **'smiling beatifically'**; the ***adverb*** **'beatifically'** means saint-like but Napoleon is behaving in the exact opposite way, signalling to the reader that Orwell is making Napoleon a figure of fun. This is only reinforced later when we find out that the bank notes are fakes and his triumph is actually a complete failure. Orwell shows us that even if a leader has complete power, it does not mean that we should respect him or her and certainly the ***satire*** here attacks Stalin. Joseph Stalin created a cult of personality that helped him maintain power through creating an impression of himself as god-like, which links to the idea of Napoleon **'smiling beatifically'**. The Russian people were used to supporting one, strong, all-powerful leader through the centuries of rule by the Tsars; this made it easier for Stalin to establish himself as an autocratic ruler, just as the animals on the farm, who were used to Jones' absolute governance, accept Napoleon's totalitarian rule.

✓ Move to the point that Orwell uses Napoleon to show us how power corrupts

The visual ***image*** of Napoleon reclining on his bank notes is an obscene ***image*** which smacks of open corruption. Yet this corruption is hinted at from the very beginning when Napoleon takes the first opportunity to personally profit from the revolution by taking control of the fresh milk: **'never mind the milk, comrades,' cried Napoleon, placing himself in front of the buckets.'** Later, the reader learns that the milk has been mixed into the pigs' mash. Even though the revolution is only hours old, Napoleon is clearly determined to benefit from the overthrow of the humans, and his cynicism and self-interest is evident from the opening. Orwell meant this incident to be a turning point in the novel, showing through the ***structure*** of the novel how the revolution is doomed even as it is beginning because of the ruthlessness of characters such as Napoleon. There is ***irony*** in the way that Napoleon addresses the other animals with the title **'comrades'** which implies complete solidarity and commitment even as he plans to betray them. We are given a sense of his physical presence by the way he puts his body **'in front of the buckets'**. We already know that he is **'large'** and there is perhaps a sense of physical threat in his action, ***foreshadowing*** how he will use violence and intimidation later on in the novel.

12   NAPOLEON   ANIMAL FARM

☑ Make the point that Napoleon wields power through deceit and violence

This violence is very soon horribly clear. Napoleon desires complete control of Animal Farm and is not interested in sharing it with Snowball; it is not long before he expels Snowball, his only real rival for power as **'nine enormous dogs wearing brass-studded collars... dashed straight for Snowball'**. The **adjectives 'enormous'** and **'brass-studded'** in the description help create a sense of violent brutality while the **verb 'dashed'** shows their speed. Napoleon has the dogs well-trained in his service and uses them ruthlessly throughout the novel to control the animals through fear and intimidation, just as Stalin used his secret police, the NKVD, to eliminate rivals and suppress dissent. Yet Napoleon does not just reply on violence to maintain control. He uses the character of Squealer to be his mouth-piece and manipulate the animals into towing the line. Napoleon uses Squealer with his skill at twisting the truth to help control the animals and Squealer alters the fifth commandment to reflect the pigs' new habit of drinking alcohol, writing **'no animal shall drink alcohol to excess'**. Napoleon and Squealer wield power through deceit and manipulation. Their literacy and the other animals' lack of education means that it is easy for Napoleon to exploit his power.

☑ Explore whether Napoleon is entirely to blame for the failure of the animals' revolution

Napoleon clearly sees Old Major's speech as a way for himself to gain control and power in the farm, not as an ideology to aspire to. He loses no time in beginning to undermine the principles of Animalism, and systematically and deliberately changes each of the commandments so that it gives him and his elite advisors more power and privileges. We wonder what would have happened if Snowball had managed to gain ultimate control over Napoleon and whether the revolution would have had a different, happier ending. However, it is not perhaps fair to lay the blame entirely on Napoleon's doorstep as there are plenty of factors that lead to Napoleon being able to take and keep control, not least the apathy and intellectual weakness of the other animals. Boxer's maxim **'Napoleon is always right'** shows a meek acceptance of his leader, an apathy which plays straight into Napoleon's hands. Orwell intended his novel to show how revolutions were almost inevitably doomed to fail with one master being exchanged for another if the working classes did not challenge their leaders. Orwell had actively participated in the Spanish Civil War, and in the process had become cynical of revolutions, especially as he observed events in the Soviet Union unfold. He believed that power corrupts, and we are given the impression that Snowball or any of the pigs who might have taken power in Napoleon's place would have ended up just as corrupt. This sense of inevitability of the corruption of a leader is evident at the end of the novel when Napoleon is walking on two legs, sleeping in a bed and is, essentially, a human; so much so that the watching animals cannot tell Napoleon and Mr Pilkington apart as **'it was impossible to say which was which'**. Napoleon's transformation into a human reflects the **cyclical structure** of the novel and shows us that the failure of the revolution was a foregone conclusion.

Essential Exam Tips

☑ Read the novel on your own at home. Try listening to an audio book as well.

☑ Refer to different places within the novel. Don't just write about the start of the novel, for example, as that doesn't show the examiner that you have a good understanding of the whole novel.

2 Snowball
Character analysis

Snowball is the intelligent pig who, with Napoleon, initially takes leadership of Animal Farm. However, this joint leadership soon leads to friction and Napoleon takes ultimate control, chasing Snowball off the farm.

'All animals are equal'

- Snowball works on Old Major's speech so that the Animalism is formed with the central concept that **'all animals are equal'**; it is Snowball who writes up the commandments on the wall.

- Snowball's zeal and belief in the revolution is seen in these principles of Animalism. There is a sense of fanaticism and power in the wording of the commandment. The **declarative sentence** is forceful and the other commandments are similar or use the **modal verb 'shall'** which implies that Snowball is imposing his will on the intellectually weaker animals.

Context: Orwell used Snowball as an **allegorical** figure for the revolutionary, Leon Trotsky, who was a main instigator of the Russian Revolution of 1917. Trotsky was a fanatic who was partly responsible for the Red Terror of 1918 when thousands of people who opposed the revolution were massacred.

'did not actually work but directed and supervised the others... 'Gee up, comrade!'

- Snowball does not become involved in the hard manual labour of the farm but takes the role of managing the other animals. Snowball's hypocrisy is evident here and undermines his professed belief that **'all animals are equal'**. There is a huge difference between the physical effort of manual labour and the much easier job of supervision which is a **'natural'** role for himself and the pigs as they are more intelligent.

- The **imperative verb 'gee'** is a clear command to the working animals and implies that Snowball and the pigs are in charge.

Context: Orwell kept farmyard animals himself and drew on his knowledge of these animals, such as the intelligence of pigs, when writing his novel.

'without halting for an instant'

- Snowball leads the charge on the attacking humans in the Battle of the Cowshed.
- The **clause** shows how brave Snowball is, with such faith in the revolution that he is willing to die for it.

Context: Like Snowball, Trotsky was a great military campaigner and was one of the founders of the Red Army.

'almost every animal on the farm was literate in some degree'

- Snowball's reading and writing classes are a success.
- His commitment to educating the animals shows Snowball in a positive light, as a leader who wishes to see all animals become empowered.
- Alternatively, Snowball's interest in education could be a clever excuse for him to build up a powerbase in his rivalry with Napoleon. This is perhaps suggested through the **third person narrative** which dispassionately notes that the animals are literate **'in some degree'**, the **determiner** 'some' indicating that the classes were not particularly successful. Maybe Snowball's real aim was to create a loyal following under the pretence of forming education classes.

'in glowing sentences, he painted a picture of Animal Farm... with electric light, hot and cold water'

- Snowball's ideas for the windmill are based on a desire for technology to improve the lives of the working animals, showing his intelligence as he plans ahead, understanding difficult concepts such as electricity.
- The **adjective** 'glowing' suggests his visionary hopes for the future as something bright and full of hope and shows him to be an articulate public speaker who is able to sway opinion. As such, he is a clear threat to Napoleon, who does not bother to debate with Snowball but sends in his vicious dogs to exterminate his brilliant rival. Snowball's eloquence contrasts with Napoleon's reticence (dislike of public speaking).

Context: Orwell fought in a Trotskyist group during the Spanish Civil War. His portrayal of Snowball, the **allegorical** figure for Trotsky, is more favourable that his portrayal of Napoleon, perhaps because of this connection.

ANIMAL FARM — SNOWBALL

> 'nine enormous dogs wearing brass-studded collars... dashed straight for Snowball'

- Snowball is expelled from the farm, chased by Napoleon's vicious dogs.
- The **adjectives** '**enormous**' and '**brass-studded**' in the description help create a sense of violent brutality while the **verb** '**dashed**' shows their speed. Napoleon has the dogs well-trained in his service and uses them ruthlessly throughout the novel to control the animals through fear and intimidation.
- **Structurally**, this is an important turning point in the story as it is the moment that Napoleon seizes complete power. With the expulsion of Snowball, Napoleon has eliminated the only serious contender for power.

> 'He stole the corn, he upset the milk-pails, he broke the eggs'

- Once expelled from the farm, Snowball is blamed for everything that goes wrong on the farm.
- Napoleon uses his old enemy to create a useful scapegoat. Snowball becomes part of Napoleon's armoury of ways in which to control the animals by demonising the absent pig into a malevolent force who is intent on destroying Animal Farm.
- The **list** here shows the range of sly, mischievous activities that Snowball is accused of, and also highlights the ridiculousness of the accusations.

Grade 9 Exploration:
Look at the character in a different way

Does the reader feel any sympathy for Snowball?

Yes: His passionate enthusiasm is almost infectious as he works to improve the farm in a way that is '**indefatigable**', showing his real determination and dedication towards the cause of animal equality. Despite the failure of many of his projects, he perseveres with success at his education programme and his bravery at the Battle of the Cowshed is remembered by the readers, if not the animals. He is altogether a more likeable, genuine leader than Napoleon and, with his eviction, the fortunes of Animal Farm turns inexorably for the worse.

No: He is ultimately as corrupt as Napoleon, taking the milk as his privilege from the very first day of the revolution. This betrayal undermines his fine words about equality and shows him to be as corrupt as any other leader in power.

As a result of his own experiences fighting during the Spanish Civil War, Orwell became disillusioned in the power or success of revolutions, seeing them simply as swapping one master for another. Snowball's presentation seems favourable compared to the brutal Napoleon but we should question whether he would have been any more resistant to the corrupting influence of power if he had stayed on the farm.

Snowball

Snowball helps found Animalism. He is fanatical in his approach to the success of the revolution.

'All animals are equal'

Snowball is a revolutionary.

His commitment to educating the animals shows Snowball in a positive light, as a leader who wishes to see all animals become empowered.

'almost every animal on the farm was literate in some degree'

Snowball is an advocate of education.

Snowball is expelled and used as a scapegoat.

'He stole the corn, he upset the milk-pails, he broke the eggs'

Snowball becomes part of Napoleon's amoury of ways in which to control the animals. Napoleon demonises Snowball.

Does the reader feel any sympathy for Snowball?

Yes: He is passionate about the revolution and we wonder if the story would have had a happier ending if he stayed on the farm.

No: His hypocrisy over the milk on the first day of the revolution completely undermines any sympathy we might have for him.

Sample GCSE Exam Question & Answer

Q: How does Orwell present the character of Snowball in his novel 'Animal Farm'?

✓ Start with the point that Snowball is presented as a revolutionary figure

Snowball is the intelligent pig who, with Napoleon, initially takes leadership of Animal Farm. Inspired by Old Major's speech, Snowball works with Napoleon and Squealer to form the ideology of Animalism, with the central concept that **'all animals are equal'**; it is Snowball who writes up the commandments on the wall. Snowball's zeal and belief in the revolution are seen in these principles of Animalism. Yet already, there is a sense of fanaticism and power in the wording of the commandment. The **declarative sentence** is forceful and the other commandments are similar or use the **modal verb 'shall'** which seems to imply that Snowball is imposing his will on the intellectually weaker animals. He comes across as fanatical in his belief in Animalism, refusing for example to allow Mollie to wear the ribbons that she loves as he sees it as contrary to the principles of Animalism. In this, he is perhaps as much a dictator as Napoleon becomes. Orwell used Snowball as an allegorical figure for the revolutionary, Leon Trotsky, who was a main instigator of the Russian Revolution of 1917 and who was passionate about the ideals of communism.

✓ Move to the point that Snowball is used to contrast with Napoleon

Snowball's passion for the revolution is seen as he defends the farm in the Battle of the Cowshed and leads the charge on the attacking humans **'without halting for an instant'**. The **clause** shows how brave Snowball is, so believing in the revolution that he is willing to die for it. Like Snowball, Trotsky was a great military campaigner and was one of the founders of the Red Army. Snowball's passion is also seen in his enthusiasm for education; his dedication is almost infectious as he works to improve the farm in a way that is **'indefatigable'**, capturing his real determination and dedication towards the cause of animal equality so that **'almost every animal on the farm was literate in some degree'**. His commitment to the education of the animals shows Snowball in a positive light, as a leader who wishes to see all animals become empowered. This marks him as different to Napoleon, whose only interest in education is to train the puppies to become killers.

✓ Continue to explore how Snowball is presented as a positive leader

This positive contrast of Snowball against the character of Napoleon might be founded in Orwell's personal experience. Orwell fought in a Trotskyist group during the Spanish Civil War and so his portrayal of Snowball, the allegorical figure for Trotsky, is more favourable that his portrayal of Napoleon, perhaps because of this connection. We again see Snowball's revolutionary zeal and also his intelligence with his ideas for the windmill which are based on a desire for technology to improve the lives of the working animals. He presents these ideas at one of the meetings as **'in glowing sentences, he painted a picture of Animal Farm... with electric light, hot and cold water'**. The **adjective 'glowing'** suggests his visionary hopes for the future as something bright and full of hope. The **metaphor 'painted a picture'** shows him to be an articulate public speaker and one who is able to sway public opinion. As such, he is a clear threat to Napoleon, who does not bother to debate with Snowball but sends in his vicious dogs to exterminate his brilliant rival. The horror of this episode is shown through the description of the **'nine enormous dogs wearing brass-studded collars... dashed straight for Snowball'**. The **adjectives 'enormous'** and **'brass-studded'** in the description help create a sense of violent brutality while the **verb 'dashed'** shows their speed. Napoleon has the dogs well-trained in his service and uses them ruthlessly throughout the novel to control the animals through fear and intimidation. **Structurally**, this is an important turning point in the story as it is the moment that Napoleon seizes complete power. With the expulsion of Snowball, Napoleon has eliminated the only serious contender for power. Yet even with Snowball banished, Napoleon uses his old enemy to create a useful scapegoat as Snowball is blamed for everything that goes wrong on the farm: '**he stole the corn, he upset the milk-pails, he broke the eggs'**. Snowball becomes part of Napoleon's armoury of ways in which to control the animals by demonising the absent pig into a malevolent force who is intent on destroying Animal Farm. The *list* here shows the range of sly, mischievous activities that Snowball is accused of and also highlights the ridiculousness of the accusations. The reader feels the injustice that the visionary Snowball has been so destroyed by brute force and lies.

✓ Explore how much sympathy the reader has for Snowball

Yet our sympathy for Snowball is, perhaps, not extensive. Snowball is by no means a hero and is, in fact, as corrupt as Napoleon, taking the milk as his privilege from the very first day of the revolution. This betrayal undermines his fine words about equality and shows him to be as corrupt as any other leader in power. We see this again in the way that he, with the other pigs, **'did not actually work but directed and supervised the others... 'Gee up, comrade'!'** Snowball's hypocrisy is evident here and undermines his professed belief that **'all animals are equal'**. There is a huge difference between the physical exhaustion of manual labour and the much easier job of supervision which is a **'natural'** role for Snowball and the pigs as they are more intelligent. The *imperative verb* **'gee'** is a clear command to the working animals and implies that Snowball and the pigs are in charge. Orwell kept farmyard animals himself and drew on his knowledge of these animals, such as the intelligence of pigs, when writing his novel. Furthermore, Snowball's virtuous interest in education could be a clever excuse for him to build up a powerbase in his rivalry with Napoleon. This is perhaps suggested through the *third person narrative* which dispassionately notes that the animals are literate **'in some degree'**, the *determiner* **'some'** indicating that the classes were not particularly successful. Maybe Snowball's real aim was to create a loyal following under the guise of education classes. As a result of his own experiences fighting in a Trotskyist group during the Spanish Civil War, Orwell became disillusioned in the power or success of revolutions; while Snowball's presentation seems favourable compared to the brutal Napoleon, we should still question whether he would have been any more resistant to the corrupting influence of power if he had stayed on the farm.

Essential Exam Tips

✓ Try to watch the cartoon version of the novel. It's quite fun and breaks up the hard work of revision.

✓ Try to weave points about context into your answer when you are writing about a character or theme. Try not to just bolt the context on at the end or add it in a completely separate paragraph.

3 Boxer & Clover
Character analysis

Boxer and Clover are the two horses whose hard work and dedication are crucial to the success of Animal Farm.

'I will work harder'

- Boxer's motto is **'I will work harder'**.
- Boxer is a determined, dedicated worker. Orwell ensures that we respect him through the use of the **modal verb 'will'** that shows his complete commitment to the success of the revolution. There are numerous examples in the novel of Boxer applying his motto by working long hours to the very limits of his strength.
- Yet this work ethic is his answer to any problems or issues that arise. His absorption in his work dulls his ability to think for himself.

Context: Boxer is used by Orwell as an **allegory** for the working class labourer in the Soviet Union. The working class helped overthrow the Tsars; their manual labour was crucial for the economic prosperity of the country and therefore the success of the revolution.

'great iron shod hoofs'

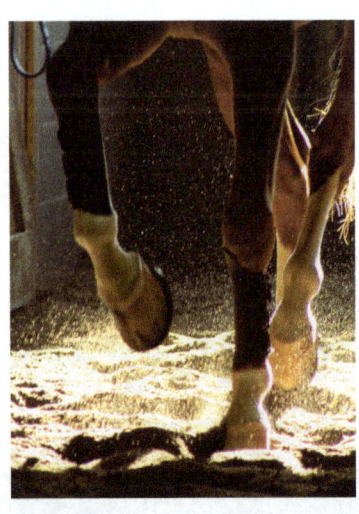

- Boxer's strength is clear in the description of his **'great iron shod hoofs'** that knock out the stable-lad at the Battle of the Cowshed.
- Boxer is capable of violence in order to defend his comrades. Yet later he regrets hurting the boy which shows that he does not enjoy violence in the way that Napoleon or the dogs do, and that he has a generous, warm nature.
- The sense of huge power in the description reminds the reader that Boxer could overthrow the pigs if he chose to as iron is an incredibly strong metal.

Context: Orwell's idea for the story came from an incident when he watched a horse being whipped, and considered how easy it would be for the horse to fight back, if it chose.

'could not get beyond the letter D'	• Boxer is unable to learn the alphabet; he **'could not get beyond the letter D'**. • Boxer is physically strong but intellectually weak. He does place value on education, planning to learn the rest of the alphabet in his retirement.	
'animals huddled about Clover'	• After the show trials and executions, the animals turn to Clover for comfort. • The **verb 'huddled'** shows how the animals seek strength and protection from Clover, drawing comfort from her maternal nature.	**Context:** Clover is a **symbol** for the female working class in Russia who played an important part in the overthrow of the Tsar. In 1917, the desperate women workers marched from their factories, demanding bread and calling for strike action.
'as Clover looked down the hillside her eyes filled with tears'	• At this point in the novel, Clover is sitting on the **'knoll'** (a small hill) overlooking the farm just after the show trials and executions. • We see here how passionately she feels for the farm, and shows how connected she is with the land.	**Context:** This reflects the strong feeling the rural Russian people had for their country.
'if she could have spoken her thoughts'	• Clover is full of despair at the horrors of the execution and struggles to articulate her disappointment at the outcome of the revolution. • The **conditional tense** here shows how she is not able to speak aloud her thoughts, perhaps showing how free speech has been shut down by Napoleon so that Clover lives in fear of speaking the truth. However, the **conditional tense** could perhaps reflect how she, like Boxer, is too intellectually weak to clearly voice her feelings. Or, perhaps, that she is limited in her communication because of her lack of education.	**Context:** Orwell was a great champion of the working classes, as seen in his novel 'The Road to Wigan Pier'. He believed that education was crucial if the working classes were to be strong enough to push for a true democratic society.

> **'But alas! His strength had left him'**

- Boxer tries to kick his way out of the horse slaughterer's van but is too weak.
- There is a strong sense of **pathos** in the once-strong Boxer who is left too weak to save himself. There is **irony** in that he has worn himself out in the cause of the revolution yet at the end the revolution completely fails him.
- The author's voice clearly directs our response to sympathy in the phrase **'but alas!'** The **exclamatory phrase** openly grieves for Boxer's inability to escape his fate and captures the tragedy that is Boxer's horrid, brutal death.
- This incident **structurally** marks another point for the reader in the story of the failure of equality. Boxer's faith in the revolution and his plans for retirement are shown to be worthless; the revolution has no use for workers who cannot work and so dispenses of them in a ruthless fashion.

Grade 9 Exploration:
Look at the characters in a different way

Are Boxer and Clover the heroes of the novel?

Yes: Clover and Boxer are steadfastly loyal and hard-working, showing great kindness to the other animals and real commitment to the ideals of Animalism. Clover is not stupid, suspecting Mollie of her defection to the humans and learning the alphabet. She and Boxer are figures that the other animals look up to; indeed, at the end, Clover is, perhaps, a **symbol** of hope. The **cyclical structure** of the novel with the pigs and humans morphing into one cruel, corrupt tyrant means that the reader wonders whether there will be another revolution; Clover is not so downtrodden that she cannot investigate what the pigs are up to. The animals creep up to the farmhouse and **'paused, half-frightened to go on, but Clover led the way in'**. The **conjunction 'but'** emphasises the courage of the old horse and her authority is clear in the **verb 'led'**. If there is to be another revolution, it will perhaps be Clover, who has witnessed the whole process already, who will be instrumental in bringing it about.

No: Far from being heroes, Boxer and Clover fail their fellow animals. They have the physical power to overturn the pigs' brutal rule yet they do nothing, blinded by propaganda and crippled with apathy. Boxer's passive acceptance of Napoleon in the end leads him to his death, as does his own weakness; if he could have got beyond the letter D, then he would have been able to read the lettering on the horse-slaughter's van. As for Clover being a **symbol** of hope, this seems unlikely as she, like the other animals, fails to challenge the pigs at any point in the novel.

Orwell's life experiences of fighting in the Spanish Civil War and also observing the events unfold in the Soviet Union made him cynical of revolutions. He believed that revolutions can only be successful if the working classes are active and engaged. Clover and Boxer are not engaged or educated enough to effectively challenge the pigs yet there are hints that this might change.

Boxer & Clover

Boxer's use of the **modal verb** 'will' shows his dedication. The pigs rely on his strength for the farm to prosper.

The **conditional tense** shows how Clover is limited through a lack of education; she is inarticulate and therefore unable to challenge the pigs.

'I will work harder'

'if she could have spoken her thoughts'

Boxer and Clover work incredibly hard in order for the revolution to succeed.

Both horses fail to challenge the pigs.

Boxer's death is one of the most painful episodes in the novel.

Are Boxer and Clover the heroes of the novel?

'But alas! His strength had left him'

Yes: They show real commitment and loyalty throughout while Clover is our only chance of hope at the end.

The **exclamatory phrase** 'but alas!' clearly directs the reader to feel the pain of the once-strong Boxer reduced to such weakness.

No: The horses do not use their strength to challenge Napoleon and so they fail the other animals.

Sample GCSE Exam Question & Answer

Q: What is the significance of Boxer and Clover in 'Animal Farm'?

☑ **Start with the point that Boxer and Clover are crucial to the success of the revolution**

Boxer and Clover are the two cart-horses whose hard work and dedication are crucial to the success of Animal Farm. Boxer is a determined, dedicated worker who takes on the motto of **'I will work harder'** to spur him on to ever greater endeavours. Orwell ensures that we respect him through the use of the **modal verb 'will'** that shows his complete commitment to the success of the revolution, and there are numerous examples in the novel of Boxer applying his motto by working long hours to the very limits of his strength. Boxer is used by Orwell as an allegory for the working class labourer in Russia. The working class helped overthrow the Tsars and their manual labour was crucial for the economic prosperity of the country; the pigs completely rely on Boxer's strength to make Animal Farm a viable concern. Similarly, Clover is an allegory for the female women workers who also played an important part in the overthrow of the Romanov Regime. In 1917, the desperate women workers marched from their factories, demanding bread and calling for strike action, and Clover represents their moral strength. For example, after the show trials and executions, the **'animals huddled about Clover'** for reassurance. The **verb 'huddled'** shows how the animals seek strength and protection from Clover, drawing comfort from her maternal nature. At this point in the novel, she is sitting on the **'knoll'** (a small hill) overlooking the farm just after the executions and **'as Clover looked down the hillside her eyes filled with tears'**. We see here how passionately she feels for the farm, showing how connected she is with the land and reflecting the strong feeling the rural Russian people have for their country.

☑ **Move to the point that both characters are very powerful**

Both characters are emotionally and physically powerful. Boxer's strength is clear in the description of his **'great iron shod hoofs'** that knock out the stable lad at the Battle of the Cowshed. Boxer is capable of violence in order to defend his comrades but later Boxer regrets hurting the boy which shows that he does not enjoy violence in the way that Napoleon or the dogs do. His compassion for the unconscious boy shows his generous, warm nature. There is the sense of huge power in the **adjective 'great'**, while iron is an incredibly strong metal. Interestingly, though, his hoofs are shod; the iron horse shoes which makes his so dangerous are placed there by man. We see even here that his power is partly given to him by his masters yet we are reminded the reader that Boxer could overthrow the pigs if he chose to. Orwell wrote in his preface to one of his editions of the novel that the idea for 'Animal Farm' came from an incident when he watched a horse being whipped and considered how easy it would be for the horse to fight back, if it chose. Yet Boxer does not choose to, or maybe he cannot, hampered by a lack of education that prevents him from understanding how to challenge the cunning and power of the pigs.

☑ **Make the point that Boxer's death is significant in documenting the failure of Animalism**

Boxer's death near the end of the novel marks perhaps the cruelest signpost in the failure of Animalism. Old and weak, Boxer is now redundant to the pigs so they callously sell him to the horse slaughterer to be boiled into glue. This dreadful end to the loyal, noble Boxer is a painful episode and the reader is horrified by the desperate struggle of Boxer to break free before it is too late. Yet he is too weak, as is clear in the lines **'but alas! His strength had left him'**. There is a strong sense of **pathos** in the once-strong Boxer left too weak to save himself. There is **irony** in that he has worn himself out in the cause of the revolution yet at the end the revolution completely fails him. The author's voice clearly directs our response to sympathy in the phrase **'but alas!'** as the **exclamatory phrase** openly grieves for Boxer's inability to escape his fate, and captures the tragedy that is Boxer's horrid, brutal death. This incident **structurally** marks another point for the reader in the catalogue of the failure of equality. Boxer's faith in the revolution and his plans for retirement are shown to be worthless; the revolution has no use for workers who cannot work and so dispenses of them in a ruthless fashion.

☑ Explore whether Boxer and Clover are significant as heroes of the novel

Clover and Boxer are steadfastly loyal and hard-working, showing great kindness to the other animals and real commitment to the ideals of Animalism. Clover is not stupid, suspecting Mollie of her defection to the humans and learning the alphabet. She and Boxer are figures that the other animals look up to; indeed, at the end, Clover is, perhaps, a **symbol** of hope. The **cyclical structure** of the novel with the pigs and humans morphing into one cruel, corrupt tyrant means that the reader wonders whether there will be another revolution; Clover is not so downtrodden that she cannot investigate what the pigs are up to. The animals creep up to the farmhouse and **'paused, half-frightened to go on, but Clover led the way in.'** The **conjunction** **'but'** emphasises the courage of the old horse and her authority is clear in the **verb 'led'**. If there is to be another revolution, it will perhaps be Clover, who has witnessed the whole process already, who will be instrumental in bringing it about. Yet there is an alternative view, that, far from being heroes, Boxer and Clover fail the other animals. They have the power to overturn the pigs' brutal rule yet they do nothing, blinded by propaganda and crippled with apathy. Boxer's passive acceptance of Napoleon in the end leads him to his death; if he could have got beyond the letter D, then he would have been able to read the lettering on the horse-slaughter's van. As for Clover being a **symbol** of hope, this seems unlikely as she, like the other animals, fails to challenge the pigs at any point in the novel. An example of this is when Clover is full of despair at the horrors of the execution and struggles to articulate her disappointment at the outcome of the revolution: **'if she could have spoken her thoughts'**. The **conditional tense** here reflects how she is not able to speak aloud her thoughts, perhaps illustrating how free speech has been shut down by Napoleon so that Clover lives in fear of speaking the truth. However, the **conditional tense** could perhaps reflect how she, like Boxer, is too intellectually weak to clearly voice her feelings. Orwell's life experiences of fighting in the Spanish Civil War and also observing the events unfold in the Soviet Union made him cynical of revolutions. He believed that revolutions can only be successful if the working classes are active and engaged. Clover and Boxer are not engaged or educated enough to effectively challenge the pigs yet there are perhaps hints that this might change.

📝 Essential Exam Tips

☑ Learn quotations off by heart. Write them out on sticky labels and put them by the kettle/on the bathroom mirror etc- places where you go to all of the time.

☑ Use the word 'Orwell'! It sounds silly but you need to write about what Orwell is doing. So use phrases such as 'Orwell presents' / 'Orwell uses'.

4 Squealer & Propaganda
Character analysis

Squealer is the pig who acts as Napoleon's loyal mouthpiece. He uses his ability to argue and persuade to help to control the animals on the farm.

'Squealer'

- Squealer's name gives us a clue to his personality. A squeal is a loud sound, showing how dominant and powerful Squealer and his oratory skills are on the farm.

- Alternatively, to **'squeal'** is a **colloquial** term which means to betray. Squealer certainly betrays the ideals of Animalism at every turn and constantly betrays his fellow animals by manipulating them into slavery.

Context: Orwell kept farmyard animals himself and would have been familiar with the squealing and squeaking of pigs.

'brilliant talker… he had a way of skipping from side to side and whisking his tail which was very persuasive'

- Squealer's power lies in his abilities as a public speaker.

- The **adjective 'brilliant'** tells the reader how expert Squealer is at talking. Part of his powers of persuasion lies in how he, like all good public speakers, uses body language to strengthen his points. Squealer's movements are quick and bewildering, shown in the **verbs 'skipping'** and **'whisking'**, designed to mesmerise and confuse the listening, watching animals.

Context: Orwell uses the character of Squealer as an **allegory** of Stalin's chief propagandist, Vyacheslav Molonov. Molonov was a polished public speaker and used hand gestures to emphasise his points.

'the others said... he could turn black into white'

- Squealer uses his powers of language to persuade the animals to believe anything.

- The use of colour opposites **'black'** and **'white'** show just how deceitful Squealer is. He has the ability to persuade the animals of the complete opposite to the truth.

- The animals know that Squealer has this ability to twist the truth yet they still believe him. This perhaps shows how the people are manipulated by government propaganda, and reflects Orwell's frustration at working class apathy that means they accept the lies fed to them by their governments.

Context: Orwell was a political writer, living and working at a time when centralised media was reaching ever greater numbers of people through more widespread availability of TV and radio. He was interested in how media was being used to influence the population.

'it is for your sake that we drink that milk and eat those apples'

- Squealer explains to the animals how it is for their benefit that the pigs are taking supplies for themselves and not sharing them with everyone.

- His use of the **pronoun 'your'**, used first in the **syntax** of the sentence, reflects the apparently selfless motives of the pigs, putting the other animals first. His **declarative statement** shows a complete certainty which convinces the animals into accepting the situation.

'No animal shall drink alcohol to excess'

- It is Squealer who changes the fifth commandment on the wall.

- Orwell uses **satire** here as Squealer changes this particular commandment while drunk, ensuring that we condemn the hypocrisy of the pigs.

- The commandments are changed throughout the story; the power of the written word is in the hands of the educated pigs, not in the hands of the animals who struggle to read.

Context: Stalin used written propaganda to control the population through the government-controlled newspaper Pravda. In the *allegorical* tale of 'Animal Farm', the written commandments and the way they are altered show how the semi-literate animals are controlled by written language.

'Surely there is no one among you who wants to see Jones back?'	• Squealer and Napoleon together use the language of fear to control the animals. • The use of **'surely'** at the start of the **rhetorical question** helps solidify the obvious answer- that of course the animals will do anything to avoid the return of the humans. The use of the **rhetorical question** convinces the animals.
'Squealer, who had unaccountably been absent'	• After the attack on the farm, Squealer appears. • His cowardice is made clear by Orwell's use of **irony**. There is nothing **'unaccountable'** about Squealer's absence; it is completely clear that he has been hiding from the fighting. • Orwell ensures that we despise the craven pig, especially as his cowardice is **contrasted** with the wounded, exhausted animals who have bravely defended the farm.

Grade 9 Exploration:
Look at the character in a different way

Is the manipulation of language Napoleon's most effective weapon?

Yes: Napoleon sees at first hand the power of language when Old Major gives his visionary speech about a land where animals are equal, inspiring the animals to rebellion. Having seen the power of language, Napoleon, who is **'not much of a talker'** himself uses the eloquent Squealer to manipulate the animals throughout. We see the huge power of language at the end when Napoleon comes out on two legs with a whip and the sheep silence any rebellion with their chant of **'four legs good, two legs better!'** Squealer's manipulation of the sheep and sly alteration of the commandment ensures that the sheep drown out and dispel the animals' protests. It is perhaps Squealer's greatest triumph as **structurally**, this is Napoleon's final corruption of the commandment and the reader sees that the revolution has completely failed.

No: Language only works so far and Napoleon needs an array of techniques to impose his will. We see this when Squealer explains about Napoleon's endorsement of Snowball's windmill; **'Squealer spoke so persuasively, and the three dogs who happened to be with him growled so threateningly'** that the animals are silenced. There is equal weight in the **syntax** of the sentence: **'so persuasively'** and **'so threateningly'**; the **repeated intensifier** and parallel **adverb** show how Napoleon uses language and violence in equal measures.

Squealer & Propagada

The animals know that Squealer has an ability to twist the truth yet they still believe him, showing how the people are manipulated by the propaganda of their leaders.

'the others said... he could turn black into white'

Squealer is briliant at manipulating language.

***

Rhetorical questions are used to control.

'Surely there is no one among you who wants to see Jones back?'

Squealer uses the language of fear.

***

Squealer uses written language.

'No animal shall drink alcohol to excess'

The commandments are changed throughout the story; the power of the written word is in the hands of the educated pigs, not in the hands of the animals who struggle to read.

***

Is propaganda Napoleon's most effective means of control?

Yes: The chanting of the sheep **'four legs good, legs *better*!'** allows Napoleon to break the final commandment; this marks the complete failure of the revolution.

No: Propaganda only works effectively when coupled with the threat of violence; Squealer walks around the farm with the growling dogs.

Sample GCSE Exam Question & Answer

Q: How does Orwell use the character of Squealer in the novel to show ideas about the power of language?

✓ **Start with the point that Squealer is a character who is expert at manipulating words**

Squealer is the character on Animal Farm who is notorious for being expert at manipulating language to ensure the dominance of the pigs. When the reader is first introduced to Squealer, Orwell tells us categorically that he is a **'brilliant talker'**, the *adjective* showing the reader how skilled Squealer is at using words. Squealer uses his powers of language to persuade the animals to believe anything; indeed, the animals said that **'he could turn black into white'**. The use of colour opposites **'black'** and **'white'** show just how deceitful Squealer is. He has the ability to persuade the animals of the complete opposite of the truth. The animals know that Squealer has this ability to twist the truth, and yet they still believe him. This perhaps shows how the people are manipulated by government propaganda and reflects Orwell's frustration at working class apathy which means that the people accept the lies fed to them by their governments. Orwell was a political writer, living and working at a time when centralised media was reaching ever greater numbers of people through the TV and radio; government leaders around the world used mass media as a way of spreading propaganda. Part of Snowball's powers of persuasion lie in how he, like all good public speakers, uses body language to strengthen his points as **'he had a way of skipping from side to side and whisking his tail which was very persuasive'**. Squealer's movements are quick and bewildering, shown in the *verbs* **'skipping'** and **'whisking'**, designed to mesmerise and confuse the listening, watching animals. Orwell uses the character of Squealer as an allegory of Stalin's chief propagandist, Vyacheslav Molonov, who was a polished public speaker and who used hand gestures to emphasise his points.

✓ **Continue to show how Squealer uses language to control the animals**

Squealer explains to the animals how it is for their benefit that the pigs are taking supplies for themselves and not sharing them with everyone, that **'it is for *your* sake that we drink that milk and eat those apples'**. His use of the *pronoun* **'your'**, used first in the *syntax* of the sentence, reflects the apparently selfless motives of the pigs, putting the other animals first. His *declarative statement* shows real certainty which convinces the animals to accept the situation. Squealer is part of the failure of the revolution from the very beginning, and his skills only improve as Squealer and Napoleon together use the language of fear to control the animals, with Squealer constantly exclaiming to any animal who questions the pigs that **'surely there is no one among you who wants to see Jones back?'** The use of **'surely'** at the start of the *rhetorical question* helps solidify the obvious answer- that of course the animals will do anything to avoid the return of the humans. The use of *rhetorical questions* is a classic technique used by propagandists to convince their listeners and Squealer, the archetypal propagandist, so controls and convinces the animals.

✓ **Move to the point that Orwell ensures that the reader despises Squealer and his skills**

There is no doubt that Squealer holds mastery over language, yet at no point does the reader admire him. It is Squealer who changes the fifth commandment on the wall to **'no animal shall drink alcohol to excess'**. Orwell uses *satire* here as Squealer changes this particular commandment while drunk, ensuring that we condemn the hypocrisy of the pigs. The commandments are changed throughout the story; the power of the written word is in the hands of the educated pigs, not in the hands of the animals who struggle to read. Stalin used written propaganda to control the population through the government-controlled newspaper Pravda. In the **allegorical** tale of 'Animal Farm', the written commandments and the way they are altered show how the semi-literate animals are controlled by written language and Orwell's use of **irony** reflects his anger at the way totalitarian leaders oppress the people that they are responsible for. Orwell's contempt for the government tool that is Squealer is very clear when, after the attack on the farm, **'Squealer, who had unaccountably been absent'** appears. His cowardice is made clear by Orwell's use of **irony**. There is nothing **'unaccountable'** about Squealer's absence; it is completely clear that he has been hiding from the fighting. Orwell ensures that we despise the craven pig, especially as his cowardice is contrasted with the wounded, exhausted animals who have bravely defended the farm.

☑ Finish with exploring whether Squealer and his gift for words are the primary means of control on the farm

Napoleon sees at first hand the power of language when Old Major gives his visionary speech about a land where animals are equal, inspiring the animals to rebellion. Having seen the power of language, Napoleon, who is **'not much of a talker'** himself, uses the eloquent Squealer to manipulate the animals throughout. We see the huge power of language at the end when Napoleon comes out on two legs with a whip and the sheep silence any rebellion with their chant of **'four legs good, two legs better!'** Squealer's manipulation of the sheep and sly alteration of the commandment ensures that the sheep drown out and dispel the animals' protests. It is perhaps Squealer's greatest triumph as, **structurally**, this is Napoleon's final corruption of the commandment and the reader sees that the revolution has completely failed. However, language only works so far and Napoleon needs an array of techniques to impose his will. We see this when Squealer explains about Napoleon's endorsement of Snowball's windmill; **'Squealer spoke so persuasively, and the three dogs who happened to be with him growled so threateningly'** that the animals are silenced. There is equal weight in the sentence structure with **'so persuasively'** and **'so threateningly'**; the **repeated intensifier** and parallel **adverb** show how Napoleon uses language and violence in equal measures, and Squealer is a key part to the success of Napoleon's brutal power-grab.

📝 Essential Exam Tips

☑ Try to embed quotations in your answer.

☑ Spend five minutes planning your answer; this helps you organise your ideas into a structure that is clear for the examiner.

5 Old Major
Character analysis

Old Major is the visionary, respected pig whose dream of a utopia where all animals are equal inspires the animals to overthrow Jones.

'Old Major... majestic-looking pig... wise and benevolent'

- Old Major is described in a positive way.
- His name suggests age and experience and also a sense of a leader; a major is a senior figure in the military.
- The **adjectives** 'majestic-looking' 'wise' 'benevolent' reinforce this sense of superiority and that he is someone who will command respect.
- He **contrasts** favourably with the drunken, irresponsible Mr Jones.

Context: Old Major is the **allegorical** figure for Karl Marx, the founder of communism.

'Remove man from the scene, and the root cause of hunger and overwork is abolished forever'

- Old Major believes that a fairer society can be achieved if humans are removed and animals are able to rule themselves.
- His argument is logical and clear: that humans are parasites who exploit the hard-working animals and, once they have been displaced, then the animals will live better, happier lives.

Context: Old Major's argument mirrors Marx's view of communism: if the social classes that are the product of capitalism are removed, then all workers will be equal and have common, shared ownership of production.

'cut your throat and boil you down'

- Old Major warns Boxer that Jones will have Boxer slaughtered once the horse is old and weak.

- Old Major is an expert orator. He uses violent language to force the animals to confront the realities of their lives. The hard-hitting **monosyllables** and the use of the clinical, functional **verbs 'cut' 'boil'** emphasise the harsh truth of Boxer's future.

- Orwell uses **foreshadowing**. Boxer will indeed suffer this fate but not from Jones: from the pigs.

'All animals are equal'

- Old Major sets out a series of statements that form the basis of Animalism.

- The clear, **declarative sentence** shows his deep belief in a fair society where everyone is equal.

- Yet already, there is a sense of fanaticism and power in his wording. The **declarative sentence** is forceful and the other commandments are similar or use the **modal verb 'shall'** which seems to imply that Old Major is imposing his will and vision on the intellectually weaker animals. This in itself perhaps undermines his ideas for an equal society.

'cruel whips no more shall crack'

- Old Major teaches the animals the 'Beasts of England' song.

- We see the need for hopes and dreams in this line which shows Jones' brutal mistreatment of his animals. From the beginning, we are on the animals' side.

- Old Major is the figure of hope at the start of the novel. He inspires the animals to examine their miserable lives and imagine a future world where they can be free from slavery and enjoy equality.

- He is an eloquent orator and shows the power of language to ignite hope. Here, the lyrics paint a picture of a world free from **'cruel whips'** that **'crack'**. The hard c consonants in the **alliteration** capture the pain of the whips that the animals endure, inspiring them to be free from their torture. Old Major's use of the **modal verb 'shall'** shows a strong level of certainty; he sees this future utopia as an event that will definitely happen and his certainty excites the animals.

# Grade 9 Exploration:
Look at the character in a different way

Is Old Major's hope for a world of equality completely unrealistic?

Yes: Old Major's dream of a world of equality is hopelessly unrealistic. He claims that the human masters are the root cause of inequality and the miseries this brings but does not recognise the failings within the animals. The desire for power within the animals is too strong and Old Major also overlooks the idea that this lust for power corrupts. We can see this through Orwell's use of positioning in the first chapter. The pigs are among the first animals to arrive and they sit down at the front of the barn, **'settled down in the straw immediately in front of the platform'**. From the outset of the story, the pigs are shown to be dominant. Their positioning of themselves at the front shows their sense of importance and privilege; this is highlighted by the deliberate use of the **adverb 'immediately'** which sharply reinforces their sense of superiority. Already, even as Old Major presents his vision for an equal society, Orwell uses the pigs' positioning to **foreshadow** how the pigs will have no interest in true equality. Even Old Major himself is **'ensconced on a raised platform'**, ostensibly so that he can communicate clearly yet the **verb 'ensconced'** suggests a permanence about this position of superiority. It is not humans who are the problem; they are simply the current masters and Orwell shows us that the desire for power will always lead to inequality and therein unhappiness.

No: Utopia is unachievable but a better, fairer society is. Orwell leaves us hope at the end of the novel that Old Major's dream will still be achievable through the character of Clover who is, perhaps, a **symbol** of hope. The **cyclical structure** of the novel with the pigs and humans morphing into one means that the reader wonders whether there will be another revolution, and certainly Clover is not so downtrodden that she cannot investigate what the pigs are up to. The animals creep up to the farmhouse and **'paused, half-frightened to go on, but Clover led the way in.'** The **conjunction 'but'** emphasises the courage of the old horse and her authority is clear in the **verb 'led'**. If there is to be another revolution, it will perhaps be Clover, who has witnessed the whole process already, who will be instrumental in bringing it about; perhaps Old Major's dream of a better, fairer society is indeed a realistic possibility.

Orwell was a great champion of the working class, as depicted in his great work 'The Road to Wigan Pier'. He believed in a more equal society that, if the working class were active and involved, could be achieved. Clover, who is the **symbol** of the working classes in the novel, can possibly instigate again that hope for a better life.

Essential Exam Tips

☑ Leave time for checking through your work. One tip is to check each paragraph as you finish it before starting the next one.

☑ You don't need to learn exactly what happens in each chapter. Referring to 'the opening' / 'when the pigs move into the farm house' etc is fine.

Old Major

Orwell's description of Old Major **contrasts** favourably to the drunken Mr Jones. The **adjectives** direct the reader to respect the elderly pig.

'majestic-looking... wise and benevolent'

Old Major gives hope at the start of the novel.

Old Major believes the the current masters, the humans, are responsible for the animals' hard lives.

'remove man from the scene'

Old Major sees self-rule as a way to a better world.

Old Major is a visionary.

'cruel whips no more shall crack'

Old Major has a dream of a future society where the animals are free and equal. He is a powerful public speaker.

Is Old Major's dream completely unrealistic?

Yes: The desire for power is too strong and will always undermine the idea of equality.

No: There might well be another revolution with a more engaged and alert working class to ensure that corruption is controlled.

Sample GCSE Exam Question & Answer

Q: What is the role of Old Major in 'Animal Farm'?

☑ Make the point that Old Major is a leader

Old Major is the visionary pig who inspires the animals to hope for a better, fairer society. Although he dies before the revolution, his influence on the animals is huge and the role he plays in the novel is a significant one. Orwell ensures that the reader sees him in a positive light through the description of Old Major as a **'majestic-looking pig'**. His name suggests age and experience and also a sense of a leader; a major is a senior figure in the military. The **adjectives 'majestic-looking' 'wise' 'benevolent'** reinforce this sense of superiority and that he is someone who will command respect. He **contrasts** favourably with the drunken, irresponsible Mr Jones and the animals are all willing to lose much needed sleep to listen to him, showing his authority and the esteem that they hold him in.

☑ Move to the point that Old Major is a visionary

It turns out that Old Major is well worth listening to as he tells the animal of his dream and the vision of a better society. Old Major believes that utopia can be achieved if humans are removed and animals are able to rule themselves. He is the figure of hope at the start of the novel as he inspires the animals to examine their miserable lives and imagine a future world where they can be free from slavery and enjoy equality. He tells them to **'remove man from the scene, and the root cause of hunger and overwork is abolished forever'**. His argument is logical and clear: that humans are parasites who exploit the hard-working animals, and, once they have been displaced, then the animals will live better, happier lives. Old Major is the allegorical figure for Karl Marx, the founder of communism. Old Major's argument mirrors Marx's view of communism: if the social classes that are the product of capitalism are removed, then all workers will be equal and have common, shared ownership of production. This idea is developed as Old Major makes a series of statements that the pigs later use to form Animalism; the most important is that **'all animals are equal'**. The clear, **declarative sentence** shows his deep belief in a fair society where everyone is equal. Yet already, there is a sense of fanaticism and power in his wording. The **declarative sentence** is forceful and the other commandments are similar or use the **modal verb 'shall'** which seems to imply that Old Major is imposing his will and vision on the intellectually weaker animals. This in itself perhaps undermines his ideas for an equal society.

☑ Make the point that Orwell uses Old Major to reflect the power of language

'Animal Farm' is a novel partly about the power of language. Orwell explores this in other novels, most notably '1984' which is set in a dystopian future where language is used to control the population. In 'Animal Farm', language is shown at first to be inspirational, and we see from the beginning of the novel how Old Major is an eloquent orator as he uses the power of language to ignite hope through the 'Beasts of England' song. One of the lines is **'cruel whips shall crack no more'**. Here, the lyrics paint a picture of a world free from **'cruel whips'** that **'crack'**. The hard c consonants in the **alliteration** capture the pain of the whips that the animals endure, inspiring them to be free from their torture. Old Major's use of the **modal verb 'shall'** shows a strong level of certainty; he sees this future utopia as an event that will definitely happen and his certainty excites the animals. He also uses the language of fear to force the animals to confront the realities of their lives when he warns Boxer that Jones will **'cut your throat and boil you down'** when Boxer becomes old and weak. The hard-hitting **monosyllables** and the use of the clinical, functional **verbs 'cut' 'boil'** emphasise the harsh truth of Boxer's future. Orwell uses **foreshadowing** here as Boxer will indeed suffer this fate but not from Jones: from the pigs.

☑ **Explore whether Orwell uses Old Major's vision to show the reader the possibility of a fairer society**

Orwell shows that Old Major's dream of a world of equality is hopelessly unrealistic. Old Major claims that the human masters are the root cause of inequality and the miseries this brings but does not recognise the failings within the animals. The desire for power is too strong and Old Major also overlooks the idea that this lust for power corrupts. We can see this through Orwell's use of positioning in the first chapter. The pigs are among the first animals to arrive and they sit down at the front of the barn, **'settled down in the straw immediately in front of the platform'**. From the outset of the story, the pigs are shown to be dominant. Their positioning of themselves at the front shows their sense of importance and privilege; this is highlighted by the deliberate use of the **adverb 'immediately'** which sharply reinforces their sense of superiority. Already, even as Old Major presents his vision for an equal society, Orwell uses the pigs' positioning to **foreshadow** how the pigs will have no interest in true equality. Even Old Major himself is **'ensconced on a raised platform'**, ostensibly so that he can communicate clearly yet the **verb 'ensconced'** suggests a permanence about this position of superiority. It is not humans who are the problem; they are simply the current masters and Orwell shows us that the desire for power will always lead to inequality and therein unhappiness. Yet, although utopia is unachievable, Orwell possibly uses Old Major to show the reader that a better, fairer society is a possibility. Orwell leaves us hope at the end of the novel that Old Major's dream will still be achievable through the character of Clover. The **cyclical structure** of the novel with the pigs and humans morphing into one means that the reader wonders whether there will be another revolution, and certainly Clover is not so downtrodden that she cannot investigate what the pigs are up to. The animals creep up to the farmhouse and **'paused, half-frightened to go on, but Clover led the way in.'** The **conjunction 'but'** emphasises the courage of the old horse and her authority is clear in the **verb 'led'**. If there is to be another revolution, it will perhaps be Clover, who has witnessed the whole process already, who will be instrumental in bringing it about; perhaps Old Major's dream of a better, fairer society is indeed a realistic possibility. Orwell was a great champion of the working class, as depicted in his great work 'The Road to Wigan Pier'. He believed in a more equal society that, if the working class were active and involved, could be achieved. Clover, who is the **symbol** of the working classes in the novel, can possibly instigate again that hope and drive for a better life and that Old Major's dream can be a reality.

Essential Exam Tips

☑ Use formal language throughout your response.

☑ Some of the exam boards will assess your spelling, punctuation and grammar on this question. Even if these skills are not assessed, you do need to write as well as you can.

6 The Minor Characters
Exploration of characters

'Animal Farm' is a story with a whole tapestry of characters who drive the plot, add engaging details and also serve as **allegorical symbols**.

'too drunk to remember to shut the pop-holes'

- Mr Jones goes to bed **'too drunk'** to remember to shut up the hen-houses.
- Orwell establishes Mr Jones from the opening sentence of the novel as an incompetent, irresponsible character who neglects his responsibilities. He ensures that we despise Jones, who is meant to be in charge of the farm, especially when he is **contrasted** with the wise and thoughtful leader that is Old Major who dominates the same chapter.

Context: Jones represents the corrupt Tsar Nicholas II who lived in luxury and neglected the needs of his people.

'easy-going gentleman-farmer' 'tough shrewd man'

- The neighbouring farmers are Mr Pilkington, an **'easy-going gentleman-farmer'** and Mr Frederick, a **'tough shrewd man'**.
- Orwell uses the farmers as **allegorical** figures. Mr Pilkington represents the countries in the capitalist West such as the United States and Great Britain, the **'easy-going'** referring to the free trade principles that mark capitalism. Mr Frederick, who is **'tough'**, represents the brutal Adolf Hitler in Germany.
- All of the humans are presented in a negative light, showing how the animals are justified in striving to be their own masters.

'Mollie refused to learn any but the five letters which spelt out her own name'

- Mollie, and the other animals, have limited interest in using their literacy skills.
- Mollie is seen as completely self-absorbed, using her skills to simply admire herself.

'Sugarcandy Mountain'

- Moses the raven is allowed back onto the farm to talk to the animals about Sugarcandy Mountain.
- The pigs allow Moses to peddle the dream of an after-life to the oppressed animals. They know that without any hope for anything better, the animals could become so disillusioned that they rebel against their new masters.

Context: Moses represents the church and reminds us of how Karl Marx claimed that 'religion is the opiate of the masses'. Certainly, we see how the animals are soothed and reassured by this hope of an after-life.

'Fools! Fools! Do you not see what is written on the side of that van?'

- Benjamin is the cynical donkey who springs into action when his friend Boxer is taken away; he shouts at the animals to try to save Boxer.
- Orwell uses Benjamin here to increase the **pathos** and drama of the scene. Benjamin is usually detached and sceptical so for him to become so animated makes us realise how dangerous Boxer's situation is.
- The **exclamatory minor sentences** 'fools! Fools' show his agitation and fear while we see his, and perhaps, Orwell's contempt at the animals' apathy that has allowed Boxer to be taken to the slaughter house.

'Four legs good, two legs better'

- The sheep's bleating silences any protest at seeing Napoleon standing on two feet with a whip.

- The sheep are grouped together to represent the working class. We have little sense of their personalities apart from their stupidity and blind obedience.

- **Structurally**, this is an important moment as the sheep allow Napoleon to break the essential principle of Animalism. The revolution is completely dead.

Context: Orwell was a great champion of the working class but his portrayal of the sheep, **symbol** of the working classes, as stupid creatures who blindly obey their leaders, suggests a contemptuous attitude. Orwell wanted 'Animal Farm' to show his readers the dangers of an inactive working class that allowed corruption amongst the ruling elite.

Grade 9 Exploration:
Look at the character in a different way

Are the minor characters simply symbols or are they convincing characters?

Symbols: The minor characters such as the humans and the majority of the animals are primarily **symbols**. Orwell deliberately gives them limited **dialogue**; indeed, the humans do not have any direct **dialogue** at all so it is difficult for us to get a sense of them as rounded, convincing characters. Furthermore, Orwell's distant, **omniscient narrative** does not allow the reader to have any insight into the minor characters' thoughts or feelings which means that it is difficult to see these characters as much more than effective symbols.

Convincing characters: Orwell presents us with an array of convincing characters who have vivid personalities. Many readers will remember Mollie's vanity as she is caught trying on Mrs Jones' ribbons and also be amused by the cat's sly attempts to use the Re-education Committee to catch birds. Orwell's skill ensures that the snapshots that we are given of the minor characters are vivid and memorable.

Orwell kept farm animals himself and used his observations of their behaviour to create realistic characters in his novel.

The Minor Characters

Jones is a drunken, cruel master and the other farmers are no better. The animals are justified in rebelling against them.

'too drunk to remember to shut the pop-holes'

The humans are all corrupt.

The sheep are grouped together to show blind obedience. They represent the working class.

'Four legs good, two legs better!'

The minor characters are *symbolic*.

The minor characters add to the drama.

'Fools! Fools! Do you not see what is written on the side of that van?'

Benjamin is spurred in to frantic activity when Boxer is taken away. His *exclamatory minor sentences* alert the reader to the danger that Boxer is in and this increases the dramatic tension and *pathos* of this scene.

Are the minor characters simply *symbols*?

Yes: The minor characters represent groups of people and Orwell's distant, *omniscient narrative* and lack of *dialogue* means that the characters serve primarily as symbols.

No: The minor characters have vivid, convincing personalities. We remember Mollie's vanity and the cat's slyness.

Sample GCSE Exam Question & Answer

Q: What do the minor characters add to the novel?
You can write about any of the minor characters such as the humans, the dogs, the sheep, the hens, Mollie, Muriel, the cat or any others.

✓ Start with the point that the minor characters add to the plot

'Animal Farm' is a story with a whole tapestry of characters who drive the plot, add engaging details and also serve as **allegorical symbols**. While characters such as the Napoleon and Boxer dominate the novel, the minor characters are crucial to the plot. An example of this is when Benjamin springs into action when his friend Boxer is taken away. Usually so detached and unemotional, in this scene he shouts at the animals to try to save Boxer, calling **'fools! Fools! Do you not see what is written on the side of that van?'** Orwell uses Benjamin here to increase the **pathos** and drama of the scene. Benjamin is usually aloof and sceptical so for him to become so animated makes us realise how dangerous Boxer's situation is. The **exclamatory minor sentences** **'fools! Fools'** show his agitation and fear while we see his, and perhaps, Orwell's contempt at the animals' apathy that has allowed Boxer to be taken to the slaughter house.

✓ Move to the point that the minor characters act as *symbols*

The minor characters do not simply serve to help drive the plot; Orwell uses them as **symbols** to represent different groups of people. Moses the raven represents the church, and although he is driven away at the start of the story by the pigs, he is allowed back onto the farm near the end to talk to the animals about Sugarcandy Mountain. The pigs permit Moses to peddle the dream of an afterlife to the oppressed animals, knowing that without any hope for anything better, the animals could become so disillusioned that they rebel against their new master. Moses reminds us of how Karl Marx claimed that 'religion is the opiate of the masses'. Certainly, we see how the animals are soothed and reassured by this hope of an after-life, and we also see the **irony** that the animals' best hope now rests in fictional place, not the in the life they fought so hard to achieve. Similarly, the farmers in the novel represent political leaders and countries. Mr Jones, who is **'too drunk to remember to shut the pop-holes'**, represents the corrupt Tsar Nicolas II while the neighbouring farmers are Mr Pilkington, an **'easy-going gentleman-farmer'** and Mr Frederick, a **'tough shrewd man'**. Mr Pilkington represents the countries in the capitalist West such as the United States and Great Britain, the **'easy-going'** referring to the free trade principles that mark capitalism. Mr Frederick, who is **'tough'**, represents the brutal Adolf Hitler in Germany. All of the humans are presented in a negative light, showing how the animals are justified in striving to be their own masters. Orwell uses these characters to highlight the message that tyranny and corruption are widespread.

✓ Make the point that the minor characters help to strengthen Orwell's messages

This message is not Orwell's only message, and, throughout the novel, he uses the minor characters to convey his political ideas. The sheep are an example of this. At the end of the novel, the sheep's bleating of **'four legs good, two legs better!'** silences any protest at seeing Napoleon standing on two feet with a whip. **Structurally**, this is an important moment as the sheep allow Napoleon to break the essential principle of Animalism and we see that the revolution is now completely dead. The sheep are grouped together to represent the working class; we have little sense of their personalities apart from their stupidity and blind obedience. Orwell was a great champion of the working class but his portrayal of the sheep, **symbol** of the working classes, as stupid creatures who blindly obey their leaders, suggests a contemptuous attitude. Orwell wanted 'Animal Farm' to show his readers the dangers of an inactive working class that allowed corruption amongst the ruling elite.

☑ **Explore whether the minor characters are *symbols* or convincing characters**

Arguably, the minor characters such as the humans and the majority of the animals are primarily **symbols**. Orwell deliberately gives them limited *dialogue*; indeed, the humans do not have any direct *dialogue* at all so it is difficult for us to get a sense of them as rounded, convincing characters. Furthermore, Orwell's distant, **omniscient narrative** does not allow the reader to have any insight into the minor characters' thoughts or feelings which means that it is difficult to see these characters as much more than effective **symbols**. Yet this is not necessarily fair. Orwell kept farm animals himself and used his observations of their behaviour to create realistic characters in his novel. He presents us with an array of convincing characters who have vivid personalities. Many readers will remember Mollie's vanity as she is caught trying on Mrs Jones' ribbons and also be amused by the cat's sly attempts to use the Re-education Committee to catch birds. Orwell's skill ensures that the snapshots that we are given of the minor characters are vivid and memorable.

Essential Exam Tips

☑ **When writing about themes, make sure you explain how the ideas affect the character and also apply to the reader.**

☑ **Exam boards use different wording for the modern text question. Check with your teacher or the exam board's website to see what sort of question your board sets**

7 Education
Exploration of a theme

The importance of education is explored throughout the story of the animals' revolution.

> 'nine puppies… Napoleon… (said) that he would make himself responsible for their education'

- Napoleon takes the puppies away to educate them.
- His version of education is to train them to obey him completely and to enjoy violence. Education is used to prop up and promote the corrupt regime.

Context: The training or indoctrination of the young was used by dictators who lived in Orwell's lifetime, such as Hitler and Stalin.

> 'almost all the animals on the farm were literate to some degree'

- Snowball's reading and writing classes are a success.
- His commitment and dedication to education of the animals shows Snowball in a positive light, as a leader who wishes to see all animals become empowered.
- This marks him as different to Napoleon, whose only interest in education is to train the puppies to become killers.
- Alternatively, Snowball's interest in education could be a clever excuse for him to build up a powerbase in his rivalry with Napoleon. This is perhaps suggested through the **third person narrative** which dispassionately notes that the animals are literate **'in some degree'**, the **determiner** **'some'** indicating that the classes were not particularly successful. Maybe Snowball's real aim was to create a loyal following under the guise of education classes. The educational initiatives might have been misused for Snowball's personal gain.

'Mollie refused to learn any but the five letters which spelt out her own name'

- Mollie, and the other animals, have limited interest in using their literacy skills.
- Mollie is seen as completely self-absorbed, using her skills to simply admire herself.

Context: Orwell was a great champion of the working class but he was frustrated by what he saw as working class apathy which ruthless leaders such as Stalin took advantage of.

'if she could have spoken her thoughts'

- Clover is full of despair at the horrors of the execution and struggles to articulate her disappointment at the outcome of the revolution.
- The **conditional tense** here captures how she is not able to speak aloud her thoughts, perhaps showing how free speech has been shut down by Napoleon so that Clover lives in fear of speaking the truth. However, the **conditional tense** could perhaps reflect how she is too intellectually weak to clearly voice her feelings. She could be unable to articulate her thoughts because of her lack of education which hampers her.

Context: Orwell saw the importance of literacy as a way of empowering the weakest in society. He believed that a literate working class would mean that the people were more likely to be politically active and therefore challenge their leaders.

'in glowing sentences, he painted a picture of Animal Farm... with electric light, hot and cold water'

- Snowball's ideas for the windmill are based on technology which will improve the lives of the working animals. He takes his ideas and builds his knowledge from books such as 'Electricity for Beginners'.
- The **adjective 'glowing'** suggests his visionary hopes for the future as something bright and full of hope. The positive **metaphor 'painted a picture'** shows how education can drastically improve a society for everyone.

ANIMAL FARM   EDUCATION

'No animal shall drink alcohol to excess'

- It is Squealer who changes the fifth commandment on the wall, showing how the principles of Animalism have been eroded and how the desire to maintain power has led to corruption.

- Orwell uses **satire** here as Squealer changes this particular commandment while drunk, ensuring that we condemn the hypocrisy of the pigs.

- The commandments are changed throughout the story; the power of the written word is in the hands of the educated pigs, not in the hands of the animals who struggle to read. We see how the revolution fails because of the pigs' superior intelligence and how they use the written word to manipulate the animals and maintain their corrupt regime.

Context: Stalin used written propaganda to control the population through the government-controlled newspaper Pravda. In the *allegorical* tale of 'Animal Farm', the written commandments and the way they are altered show how the semi-literate animals are also controlled by written language.
Orwell himself wrote propaganda for the Allies during WW2 so he knew its power at first hand.

Grade 9 Exploration:
Look at the theme in a different way

Does Orwell show us that education is the best way to a more equal society?

Yes: Orwell clearly shows us the value of education in a society which wishes to be free and equal. As a democratic socialist, he was a champion of the working class and believed that true equality would come if the workers took an interest in their own government. Perhaps the best example of this is Boxer's death. The semi-literate animals wave goodbye to Boxer as he disappears in the knacker's van, unable to read the lettering which clearly tells them his fatal destination. It is the educated Benjamin who tells them the truth, shouting **'fools! Fools! Do you not see what is written on the side of that van?'** Despite his ability to read the letters, Benjamin is too late to stop Boxer's death, partly because of the slowness and ignorance of the other animals. The reader feels the **pathos** of Boxer's death in the dour Benjamin's unusual animation; his **repetition** of **'fools'** shows his anger at their lack of literacy which contributes to the death of the noble Boxer. **Structurally**, the reader sees the dangers of illiteracy and how it leads to corrupt regimes.

No: Education can be used as a tool for the cruel and the powerful. When the animals are about to protest against Napoleon walking on his hind legs, the sheep silence any protest with their bleating **'four legs good, two legs *better*'**. They have been educated to become a puppet of the state, given a smattering of knowledge in order to peddle the government's propaganda and prop up a corrupt regime.

Education

His version of education is to train the dogs to obey him and to enjoy violence. Education is used to prop up and promote the corrupt regime.

'nine puppies... Napoleon... (said) that he would make himself responsible for their education'

Napoleon uses education as a way of gaining power.

Snowball is keen to educate all of the animals on the farm.

'almost all the animals on the farm were literate to some degree'

Snowball is passionate about education.

Education offers great possibilities.

'in glowing sentences, he painted a picture of Animal Farm... with electric light, hot and cold water'

The *adjective* 'glowing' suggests his visionary hopes for the future as something bright and full of hope. The positive language shows how education can drastically improve a society for everyone.

Does Orwell show us that education is the best way to a more equal society?

Yes: Orwell shows us the dangers of illiteracy through the pain of Boxer's death.

No: Napoleon uses education to prop up his regime by giving the sheep limited knowledge.

Sample GCSE Exam Question & Answer

Q: How does Orwell present ideas about education in 'Animal Farm'?

✓ Start with the point that education is important in terms of gaining power

The importance of education is explored throughout the story of the revolution. Attitudes towards education amongst the animals vary and Orwell uses these attitudes to examine how literacy is closely linked to power. The naturally intelligent pigs understand that literacy can be a tool for the powerful; Napoleon takes the puppies away to educate them, saying **'that he would make himself responsible for their education'**. His version of education is to train them to obey his completely and to enjoy violence, and here we see through the puppies' training into brutal dogs how education is used to promote a corrupt regime. The training or indoctrination of the young was used by dictators who lived in Orwell's lifetime, such as Hitler and Stalin. Napoleon's view on education is different to Snowball's. Snowball' s reading and writing classes are a real success so that **'almost all the animals on the farm were literate to some degree'**. His commitment and dedication to the education of the animals show Snowball in a positive light, as a leader who wishes to see all animals become empowered. This marks him as different to Napoleon, whose only interest in education is to train the puppies to become killers. Alternatively, Snowball's interest in education could be a clever excuse for him to build up a powerbase in his rivalry with Napoleon. This is perhaps suggested through the **third person narrative** which dispassionately notes that the animals are literate **'in some degree'**, the **determiner 'some'** indicating that the classes were not particularly successful and this is acceptable. Maybe Snowball's real aim was to create a loyal following under the guise of education classes. Perhaps in both leaders we see how education is used to gain and hold onto power.

✓ Move to the point that the workers are rendered powerless without education

Certainly, the animals' lack of education makes it easy for the pigs to take control as the animals are unable to express themselves. After the horrors of the show trials and executions, Clover is full of despair and struggles to articulate her disappointment at the outcome of the revolution: **'If she could have spoken her thoughts'**. The **conditional tense** here shows how she is not able to speak aloud her thoughts, perhaps showing how free speech has been shut down by Napoleon so that Clover lives in fear of speaking the truth. However, the **conditional tense** could perhaps reflect how she is too intellectually weak to clearly voice her feelings and we see how the working classes are limited if not given proper access to education. As a champion of the working class, Orwell saw the importance of literacy as a way of empowering the weakest in society yet he was frustrated by what he saw as working class apathy which ruthless leaders such as Stalin took advantage of. An example of this is in the depiction of Mollie who does not appreciate her chance to be educated and who **'refused to learn any but the five letters which spelt out her own name'**. It seems that education is not an answer in itself to enabling the populace to become empowered.

✓ Continue to explore how the leaders use their literacy as a means of control

While the animals are restricted by their lack of education, the pigs move quickly to exploit their literacy skills and we see how the revolution partly fails because of the pigs' superior intelligence and how they use the written word to manipulate the animals and maintain their corrupt regime. It is Squealer who changes the fifth commandment on the wall, writing that **'no animal shall drink alcohol to excess'** and so showing how far the principles of Animalism have been eroded and how the desire to maintain power has led to blatant corruption. Orwell uses **satire** here as Squealer changes this particular commandment while drunk, ensuring that we condemn the hypocrisy of the pigs. The commandments are changed throughout the story; the power of the written word is in the hands of the educated pigs, not in the hands of the animals who struggle to read. Stalin used written propaganda to control the population through the government-controlled newspaper Pravda. In the **allegorical** tale of 'Animal Farm', the written commandments and the way they are altered show how the semi-literate animals are controlled by written language. Orwell himself wrote propaganda for the Allies during WW2 so he knew its power at first hand.

☑ Explore whether Orwell shows us that education is the best way to a more equal society

Orwell clearly shows us the value of education in a society which wishes to be free and equal. As a democratic socialist, he believed true equality would come if the workers took an interest in their own government and education was key to this. Perhaps the best example of this is Boxer's death. The semi-literate animals wave goodbye to Boxer as he disappears in the knacker's van, unable to read the lettering which clearly tells them his fatal destination. It is the educated Benjamin who tells them the truth, shouting **'fools! Fools! Do you not see what is written on the side of that van?'** Despite his ability to read the letters, Benjamin is too late to stop Boxer's death, partly because of the slowness and ignorance of the other animals. The reader feels the **pathos** of Boxer's death in the dour Benjamin's unusual animation; his **repetition** of **'fools'** shows his anger at their lack of literacy which contributes to the death of the noble Boxer. **Structurally**, the reader sees the dangers of illiteracy and how it leads to corrupt regimes. Similarly, we see how education can be used for the good of all in Snowball's ideas for the windmill which are based on technology and which aim to improve the lives of the working animals. He takes his ideas and builds his knowledge from books such as 'Electricity for Beginners' and **'in glowing sentences, he painted a picture of Animal Farm...with electric light, hot and cold water'**. The **adjective** **'glowing'** suggests his visionary hopes for the future as something bright and full of hope. The positive **metaphor** **'painted a picture'** shows how education can drastically improve a society for everyone. Yet education is not always a force for the good, and indeed, can be used as a tool for the cruel and the powerful. When the animals are about to protest against Napoleon walking on his hind legs, the sheep silence protest with their bleating **'four legs good, two legs *better*'**. They have been educated to become a puppet of the state, given a smattering of knowledge in order to peddle the government's propaganda and prop up a corrupt regime. Perhaps the message that Orwell is hoping to give to his readers is that education must become a priority for all if it is to be used for the good of society and not as a tool for corrupt leaders.

📝 Essential Exam Tips

☑ If you can use the correct literary terminology, do! However, if you're not sure whether a word is a verb, adjective, adverb or noun, don't guess. Just write 'the word'.

☑ Don't just label a quotation as a 'simile' 'verb' etc. Explain the effect of the language: what it shows about a character or a theme and how the reader's response is affected by the language.

8 Power & Corruption
Exploration of a theme

Orwell uses his novel 'Animal Farm' to explore ideas about corruption and power in the human world.

'All animals are equal'

- One of the founding ideals of Animalism is that **'all animals are equal'**.

- At the start of the novel, the animals live in miserable servitude under the complete power of the corrupt, lazy farmer Mr Jones. In his speech, Old Major gives the animals hope for a better future, one where they are equal and free.

- There is an inspirational strength in the strong, **declarative statement**. It is definitive, with the **determiner 'all'** encompassing the whole of society as equals, with no one in a position of superiority or power.

Context: 'Animal Farm' is an **allegory** of Russia. The start of the novel mirrors the inspirational Karl Marx, who is represented by Old Major, setting out the ideas of communism. These ideas were later used by Lenin to encourage the Russian workers to rise up against the corrupt Romanov regime which wielded absolute power over the people.

'pigs... settled down in the straw immediately in front of the platform'

- The pigs are among the first animals to arrive and they sit down at the front of the barn.

- From the outset of the story, the pigs are shown to be dominant. Their positioning of themselves at the front shows their sense of importance and privilege; this is highlighted by the deliberate use of the **adverb 'immediately'** which sharply reinforces their sense of superiority.

- Already, even as Old Major presents his vision for an equal society, Orwell uses the pigs' positioning to **foreshadow** how the pigs have a sense of leadership and authority amongst the animals which will lead to them taking power.

'Never mind the milk, comrades' cried Napoleon, placing himself in front of the buckets'

- Napoleon takes the milk and later mixes it into the pigs' mash.
- Even though the revolution is only hours old, the pigs take the first opportunity to benefit from the overthrow of the humans. Their cunning and their position as natural leaders on the farm means that they are able to exploit the situation to their advantage.
- Orwell meant this incident to be a turning point in the novel, showing through the **structure** of the novel how the dream of the revolution is doomed even as it is beginning because of the desire for power and control.

Context: Orwell was a political writer who often used his novels to explore ideas of power within society. He was aware of how a position of power can lead to abuse and clearly did not enjoy holding power over others; he joined the Indian Imperial Police when he was young but left after only a few years, stating that the experience had cemented his dislike of authority.

'nine enormous dogs wearing brass-studded collars... dashed straight for Snowball'

- Snowball is expelled from the farm, chased by Napoleon's vicious dogs.
- The **adjectives** **'enormous'** and **'brass-studded'** in the description help create a sense of violent brutality while the **verb** **'dashed'** shows their speed. Napoleon has the dogs well-trained in his service and uses them ruthlessly throughout the novel to control the animals through fear and intimidation.

Context: Stalin used a brutal secret police to control the Soviet Union; the dogs represent this police squad, the NKVD. Power is achieved through terror.

'Smiling beatifically, and wearing both his decorations, Napoleon reposed... with the money at his side'

- Napoleon triumphantly displays the money he has received for the timber.
- Napoleon maintains power through creating a 'cult of personality', forcing the animals to idolise him. Orwell uses **satire** through the ironic use of the **adverb** **'beatifically'** to make fun of Napoleon and to warn the reader how we should be wary of our leaders and their manipulative ways.

> 'No animal shall drink alcohol to excess'

- It is Squealer who changes the fifth commandment, showing how far the principles of Animalism have been eroded and how the desire to maintain power has led to blatant corruption.
- Orwell uses **satire** here as Squealer changes this particular commandment while drunk, ensuring that we condemn the hypocrisy of the pigs.
- The commandments are changed throughout the story; the power of the written word is in the hands of the educated pigs, not in the hands of the animals who struggle to read, and the pigs abuse this to maintain control.

Grade 9 Exploration:
Look at the theme in a different way

Does Orwell show us a world where it is inevitable that power corrupts?

Yes: The historian Lord Acton said, 'Power tends to corrupt but absolute power corrupts absolutely' and it would seem that Orwell reflects this idea in 'Animal Farm'. Jones holds complete power over the animals and abuses this position, treating them with contempt and cruelty. Even though the revolution was supposed to bring equality, the pigs waste no time in abusing their position as leaders and the rest of the novel chronicles the erosion of the ideals of Animalism as Napoleon takes more and more power. The other animals are too naive to stop them; Boxer's maxim **'Napoleon is always right'** illustrates the mob mentality which allows leaders to exert complete authority. The other farms in the novel are equally corrupt with Pilkington and Frederick abusing their power; if the world of 'Animal Farm' is a reflection of the human world, then it would seem that power only brings with it corruption and abuse. The **cyclical structure** of the novel shows how the animals simply swap one abusive master for another, and reflects the inevitable corrupting nature of power.

No: There are characters in the novel who do not allow power to corrupt them. There is the inspirational figure of Old Major who uses his position as a leader to inspire a revolution founded on equality, while Snowball is also a champion of the workers with his committees designed to improve their lives. We see the bravery of the young porkers who protest against Napoleon's power grab even though they stand to gain from it. We also see how Boxer, despite his enormous strength, never uses this natural power in an aggressive or selfish way. Despite the dominance of Napoleon and the ending where we see how the animals have switched one abusive master for another, there is hope that power will one day be in the hands of many and that there is enough human decency to ensure that this power is not corrupted.

Orwell lived at a time when Europe had ample dictators- Stalin, Franco, Mussolini, Hitler- and was horrified at the way these men used their power. He himself was a great believer in democracy where power is given to the people and therefore the possibility for power to corrupt is tempered.

Power & Corruption

Foreshadowing is used to show how the pigs have a natural desire to be leaders and in control.

↓

'pigs... settled down in the straw immediately in front of the platform'

↓

Desire for power is a powerful motivator.

Even though the revolution is only hours old, the pigs use their position of power for their own advantage. We see how quickly power corrupts.

↓

'Never mind the milk, comrades!'

↓

Power corrupts the leaders.

Power is maintained through violence.

↓

'nine enormous dogs wearing brass-studded collars... dashed straight for Snowball'

↓

Napoleon uses violence to seize complete control and then continues to use terror as a way of maintaining power.

Does Orwell show us a world where it is inevitable that power corrupts?

↓

Yes: The *cyclical structure* of the novel shows how the animals simply swap one abusive master for another.

↓

No: There are characters within the novel such as Old Major and Boxer who do not let their power corrupt and Orwell holds out some hope that power will one day be in the hands of the many.

Sample GCSE Exam Question & Answer

Q: Write about how Orwell explores ideas about power and corruption in 'Animal Farm'.

☑ **Start with the point that the desire for power is evident from the opening**

Orwell uses 'Animal Farm' to explore ideas about corruption and power in the human world, showing us how the desire for power is an incredibly powerful motivator and also how power has a corrupting influence on the characters. At the start of the novel, the animals live in miserable servitude under the complete power of the corrupt, lazy farmer Mr Jones. In his speech, Old Major gives the animals hope for a better future, one where they are equal and free. There is an inspirational strength in the strong, ***declarative statement*** 'all animals are equal'. It is definitive, with the ***determiner*** 'all' encompassing the whole of society as equals, with no one in a position of superiority or power. 'Animal Farm' is an ***allegory*** of Russia and the start of the novel mirrors the inspirational Karl Marx, who is represented by Old Major, setting out the ideas of communism which later Lenin used to encourage the Russian workers to rise up against the corrupt Romanov regime. Yet, from the outset of the story, the pigs are shown to be dominant. They are among the first animals to arrive and they **'settled down in the straw immediately in front of the platform'**. Their positioning of themselves at the front shows their sense of importance and privilege; this is highlighted by the deliberate use of the ***adverb*** 'immediately' which sharply reinforces their sense of superiority. Already, even as Old Major presents his vision for an equal society, Orwell uses the pigs' positioning to ***foreshadow*** how the pigs have a sense of leadership and authority amongst the animals.

☑ **Make the point that power immediately begins to corrupt the leaders**

When the revolution does come, the reader's uneasy expectation that the pigs will assume leadership is borne out. Even though the revolution is only hours old, the pigs take the first opportunity to benefit from the overthrow of the humans, seizing the tasty milk for themselves. **'Never mind the milk, comrades' cried Napoleon, placing himself in front of the buckets'** and later the reader learns that the milk has been mixed into the pigs' mash. Their cunning and their position as natural leaders on the farm mean that they are able to exploit the situation to their advantage. Orwell meant this incident to be a turning point in the novel, showing through the ***structure*** of the novel how the dream of the revolution is doomed even as it is beginning because of the self-interest of the leaders. There is irony in the way that Napoleon addresses the other animals with the title **'comrades'** which implies complete solidarity even as he plans to betray them. We are given a sense of his physical presence by the way he puts his body **'in front of the buckets'**. We already know that he is **'large'** and there is perhaps a sense of physical threat in his action, ***foreshadowing*** how he will use violence and intimidation later on in the novel to achieve power. Napoleon is the ***allegorical*** figure for Stalin, the brutal dictator who used the revolution to take complete control of Russia. Just as Stalin manipulated the revolution, so does Napoleon, showing how the dream of equality is quickly eroded as the lust for power takes over.

☑ **Make the point that power continues to corrupt**

Nobody challenges Napoleon about the milk and so he is able to take more and more power. Eventually, he uses his **'nine enormous dogs wearing brass-studded collars'** to expel his only rival for power as the dogs **'dashed straight for Snowball'**. The ***adjectives*** 'enormous' and **'brass-studded'** in the description help create a sense of violent brutality while the ***verb*** 'dashed' shows their speed. ***Structurally***, this is an important turning point in the story as it is the moment that Napoleon seizes complete control of the farm. With the expulsion of Snowball, Napoleon has eliminated the only serious contender for leadership and ensures that there is now no check on his own ambitions for power. This mirrors Stalin's eliminination of his rival Trotsky from the Soviet Union. Throughout the novel, Napoleon continues to use his well-trained dogs to control the animals through fear and intimidation. He also uses the power of language to maintain his position, rewriting the commandments and so controlling the semi-literate animals. As the story develops, Napoleon and the pigs ever more blatantly abuse their position of authority. While the animals live on low rations and working incredibly long hours, the ruling elite take all of the wealth from the farm. Napoleon triumphantly displays the money he has received in payment for the timber: '**smiling beatifically, and wearing both his decorations, Napoleon reposed...with the money at his side'**. Here, we see Napoleon maintain power through creating a 'cult of personality'. This means that he deliberately projects an image of himself to the population that is revered by them. This victory celebration which he takes part in shows not just his love of power and desire to lord it over the other animals, it also shows a cunning understanding of how power works. By flaunting himself, Napoleon ensures that the other animals visibly see him as superior and also, as participants, they are passively accepting his position of authority. This is a technique used by dictators throughout history and certainly used by Stalin who was idolised by the Russian working class. Orwell uses **satire** in the image of Napoleon **'smiling beatifically'** as the **adverb 'beatifically'** means saint-like when Napoleon is behaving in the exact opposite way. This signals to us that Orwell is making Napoleon a figure of fun and this is reinforced later when we find out that the bank notes are fakes. Orwell shows us that even if a leader has complete power, it does not mean that we should respect him or her; indeed, we despise the way Napoleon has become so corrupted and so is operating far from the ideals of Animalism.

✓ Explore whether Orwell shows us a world where it is inevitable that power corrupts

The historian Lord Acton said, 'Power tends to corrupt but absolute power corrupts absolutely' and it would seem that Orwell reflects this idea in 'Animal Farm'. Jones holds complete power over the animals and abuses this position, treating them with contempt and cruelty. Even though the revolution was supposed to bring equality, the pigs waste no time in abusing their position as leaders and the rest of the novel chronicles the erosion of the ideals of Animalism as Napoleon takes more and more power. The other animals are too naive to stop them; Boxer's maxim **'Napoleon is always right'** illustrates the mob mentality which allows leaders to exert complete authority. The other farms in the novel are equally corrupt with Pilkington and Frederick abusing their power; if the world of 'Animal Farm' is a reflection of the human world, then it would seem that power only brings with it corruption and abuse. Orwell lived at a time when Europe had ample dictators- Stalin, Franco, Mussolini, Hitler- and was horrified at the way these men used their power. He himself was a great believer in democracy where power is given to the people and was aware of how a position of power can lead to abuse. He clearly did not enjoy holding power over others; interestingly, he joined the Indian Imperial Police when he was young but left after only a few years, stating that the experience had cemented his dislike of authority. Yet Orwell's message is not wholly bleak about the corrupting influence of power as there are characters in the novel who do not allow power to change them. There is the inspirational figure of Old Major who uses his position as a leader to inspire a revolution founded on equality stating clearly that **'all animals are equal'** while Snowball is also a champion of the workers with his committees designed to improve their lives. We see the bravery of the young porkers who protest against Napoleon's power grab even though they stand to gain from it. We also see how Boxer, despite his enormous strength, never uses this natural power in an aggressive or selfish way. Despite the dominance of Napoleon and the ending where we see how the animals have simply switched one abusive master for another, there are strands of hope that power will one day be in the hands of many and that there is enough human decency to ensure that this power is not corrupted.

9 Hopes & Dreams
Exploration of a theme

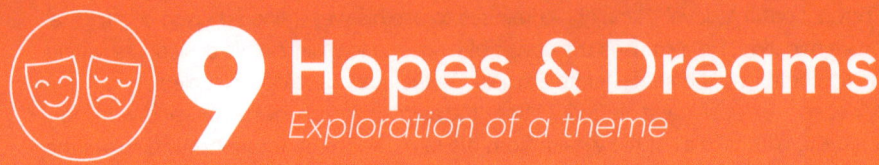

'Animal Farm' is a story of dashed hopes as the reader follows the gradual erosion of the animals' dream of a place where everyone can be equal.

'cruel whips no more shall crack'

- Old Major teaches the animals the 'Beasts of England' song.

- We see the need for hopes and dreams in this line which shows Jones' brutal mistreatment of his animals. From the beginning, we are on the animals' side.

- Old Major is the figure of hope at the start of the novel. He inspires the animals to examine their miserable lives and imagine a future world where they can be free from slavery and enjoy equality.

- He is an eloquent orator, using the power of language to ignite hope. Here, the lyrics paint a picture of a world free from **'cruel whips'** that **'crack'**. The hard c consonants of the **alliteration** capture the pain of the whips that the animals endure, inspiring them to be free from their torture. Major's use of the **modal verb 'shall'** shows a strong level of certainty; he sees this future utopia as an event that will definitely happen and his certainty excites the animals.

Context: Old Major is the **allegorical** figure that Orwell uses for Karl Marx. Karl Marx was the founder of communism, the philosophy that everyone should be equal, and Lenin used these ideas to inspire the Russian peasantry that life could be better and to rebel against the corrupt Tsars.

'pigs... settled down in the straw immediately in front of the platform'

- The pigs are among the first animals to arrive and they sit down at the front of the barn.

- From the outset of the story, the pigs are shown to be dominant. Their positioning of themselves at the front shows their sense of importance and privilege; this is highlighted by the deliberate use of the **adverb** **'immediately'** which sharply reinforces their sense of superiority.

- Already, even as Old Major presents his vision for an equal society, Orwell uses the pigs' positioning to **foreshadow** how the pigs have no interest in a dream of equality.

'they gambolled round and round, they hurled themselves into the air'

- As the humans flee after the revolution, the animals experience great joy as their dream comes true, leaping round the farm that is now theirs.

- The **dynamic verbs** of **'gambolled'** and **'hurled'** show the animals' overwhelming excitement and the hopeful enthusiasm with which they embrace their future.

- There is a sense of community here as the animals are described collectively, as one being- the animals. This reflects the camaraderie and equality which is the hallmark of their dream.

Context: Orwell originally called his novel 'Animal Farm; a fairy tale'. There is a sense of a fairy tale here with the talking, emotional animals and their extraordinary achievement. Yet the novel is also an **allegory** and any reader aware of the history of the Russian Revolution would understand this, and also be aware that the euphoria of the animals will be short-lived.

'Smiling beatifically, and wearing both his decorations, Napoleon reposed... with the money at his side'

- The use of a cult of personality is a way of keeping dreams alive as Napoleon triumphantly displays the money that he has received in payment for the timber.

- As conditions on the farm deteriorate under the pigs' rule, the animals cling determinedly to the dream of the revolution having achieved a better life and the pigs work hard to maintain that illusion.

- Napoleon's display is a way of keeping the animals' pride and dreams about Animal Farm alive; his status as a great, revered leader manipulates the animals so that they believe they are still better off under his regime than under Jones'.

ANIMAL FARM — HOPES & DREAMS

'Sugarcandy Mountain'

- Moses the raven returns to the farm to talk to the animals about Sugarcandy Mountain.
- The pigs allow Moses to peddle the dream of an afterlife to the oppressed animals. They know that without any hope for anything better, the animals could become disillusioned with their conditions and so rebel.
- It is ironic that the animals' best hope now rests in an afterlife, not the in the life they fought so hard to achieve.

Context: Moses represents the church and reminds us of how Karl Marx claimed that 'religion is the opiate of the masses'. Certainly, we see how the animals are soothed and reassured by this hope of an after-life.

Grade 9 Exploration:
Look at the theme in a different way

Does Orwell leave us with any hope for a fairer, more egalitarian society?

Yes: At the end, Clover is, perhaps, a **symbol** of hope. The **cyclical structure** of the novel with the pigs and humans morphing into one means that the reader wonders whether there will be another revolution, and certainly Clover is not so downtrodden that she cannot investigate what the pigs are up to. The animals creep up to the farmhouse and **'paused, half-frightened to go on, but Clover led the way in.'** The **conjunction** **'but'** emphasises the courage of the old horse and her authority is clear in the **verb** **'led'**. If there is to be another revolution, it will perhaps be Clover, who has witnessed the whole process already, who will be instrumental in bringing it about.

No: Napoleon's transformation into a human who has complete control over the animals reflects the **cyclical structure** of the novel and shows us that the hopes and dreams of the animals are now utterly destroyed. It seems unlikely that Clover, with her **'old, dim eyes'** can be a **symbol** of hope; she is physically frail and she, like the other animals, fails to challenge the pigs at any point in the novel. It seems that the negativity that Benjamin expresses is the underlying message of Animal Farm; Benjamin says that **'life would go on as it had always gone on- that is, badly.'** The donkey has no faith that society will ever change and his pessimism is, perhaps, our lasting message from the novel.

Orwell was a great champion of the working class, as depicted in his great work 'The Road to Wigan Pier'. He believed in a more equal society that, if the working class were active and involved, could be achieved. Clover, who is the **symbol** of the working classes in the novel, can instigate again that hope for a better life.

58   HOPES & DREAMS   ANIMAL FARM

Hopes & Dreams

Old Major gives the animals the hope of a kinder, fairer society.

'cruel whips no more shall crack'

Old Major tells the animals of his dream.

Orwell uses **foreshadowing** to warn the reader that the dream will be hard to achieve or sustain.

'pigs... settled down in the straw immediately in front of the platform'

The dream is undermined from the beginning.

Moses gives the animals hope in an afterlife.

'Sugarcandy Mountain'

It is ironic that the animals' best hope lies in a fictional place rather than the farm that they fought so hard for.

Does Orwell leave us with any hope for a fairer society?

Yes: Clover is a **symbol** for hope; she **'led'** the way up to the farm house, suggesting another revolution with a happier outcome is still possible.

No: The **cyclical structure** of the novel shows us how hopes and dreams are invitably doomed to be destroyed.

Sample GCSE Exam Question & Answer

Q: How does Orwell present the importance of hopes and dreams in 'Animal Farm'?

✓ **Start with the point that 'Animal Farm' presents the reader with a dream that seems achievable**

'Animal Farm' is a story of dashed hopes as Orwell takes the reader through the gradual erosion of the animals' dream of a place where everyone can be equal. Yet at the start of the novel, we have real belief that the animals' dream can come true. Old Major teaches the animals the 'Beasts of England' song; one of the lines is **'cruel whips no more shall crack'**. Through this line, we see the need for hopes and dreams to escape Jones' brutal mistreatment of his animals. From the beginning, we are on the animals' side. Old Major is the figure of hope at the start of the novel. He inspires the animals to examine their miserable lives and imagine a future world where they can be free from slavery and enjoy equality. He is an eloquent orator and uses the power of language to ignite hope. Here, the lyrics paint a picture of a world free from **'cruel whips'** that **'crack'**. The hard c consonants of the *alliteration* capture the pain of the whips that the animals endure, inspiring them to be free from their torture. Old Major's use of the *modal verb* **'shall'** shows a strong level of certainty; he sees this future utopia as an event that will definitely happen and his certainty excites the animals. Old Major is the *allegorical* figure that Orwell uses for Karl Marx. Karl Marx was the founder of communism, the philosophy that everyone should be equal, and as such inspired the Russian peasantry that life could be better and to rebel against the repressive Romanov regime. The revolution, inspired by this speech, comes swiftly and, as the humans flee after the revolution, the animals experience great joy as their dream comes true: **'they gambolled round and round, they hurled themselves into the air'**. The *dynamic verbs* of **'gambolled'** and **'hurled'** show the animals' overwhelming excitement and the hopeful enthusiasm with which they embrace their future. There is a sense of community here as the animals are described collectively, as one being- the animals. This reflects the camaraderie and equality which is the hallmark of their dream. Orwell originally called his novel 'Animal Farm; a fairy tale' and there is a sense of a fairy tale here with the talking, emotional animals and their extraordinary achievement.

✓ **Move to the point that there are hints from the beginning that the dream will be destroyed**

Although 'Animal Farm' can be read as a fairy tale, it can also be read as an *allegory*, and any reader aware of the history of the Russian Revolution would understand this and also be aware that the euphoria of the animals will be short-lived. Indeed, even in the opening chapter there are hints that the dream of an equal, fair society will be difficult to achieve through the presentation of the pigs, who are among the first animals to arrive, sitting down in a prominent spot as they **'settled down in the straw immediately in front of the platform'**. From the outset of the story, the pigs are shown to be dominant. Their positioning of themselves at the front shows their sense of importance and privilege; this is highlighted by the deliberate use of the *adverb* **'immediately'** which sharply reinforces their sense of superiority. Already, even as Old Major presents his vision for an equal society, Orwell uses the pigs' positioning to *foreshadow* how the pigs have no interest in a dream of equality.

✓ **Move to the point that the pigs exploit ideas of hope and dreams for their own benefit**

As conditions on the farm deteriorate under the pigs' rule, the animals cling determinedly to the dream of the revolution bringing a better life, and the pigs work hard to maintain that illusion. The use of a cult of personality is one of these ways of keeping dreams alive as Napoleon triumphantly displays the money that he has received in payment for the timber: **'smiling beatifically, and wearing both his decorations, Napoleon reposed... with the money at his side'**. Napoleon's status as a great, revered leader manipulates the animals so that they believe they are still better off under his regime than under Jones'. Near the end of the story, Moses the raven comes back onto the farm to talk to the animals about **'Sugarcandy Mountain'**. The pigs allow Moses to peddle the dream of an after-life to the oppressed animals as they know that, without any hope for anything better, the animals could become so disillusioned that they end up rebelling. It is ironic that the animals' best hope now rests in an afterlife, not the in the life that they fought so hard to achieve. Moses represents the church and reminds us of how Karl Marx claimed that religion is the opiate of the masses. Certainly, we see how the animals are soothed and reassured by this hope of an afterlife, just as the Russian Orthodox Church was used by Stalin in the 1940s to improve morale during the hard years of the war.

✓ Finish with exploring whether the novel leaves us any hope for those who dream of a fairer, more egalitarian society

Despite the conclusion of the novel with the animals living a life of miserable servitude under the complete control of Napoleon, there is perhaps, a **symbol** of hope in the character of Clover. The **cyclical structure** of the novel with the pigs and humans morphing into one means that the reader wonders whether there will be another revolution; Clover is not so downtrodden that she cannot investigate what the pigs are up to. The animals creep up to the farmhouse and **'paused, half-frightened to go on, but Clover led the way in.'** The **conjunction 'but'** emphasises the courage of the old horse and her authority is clear in the **verb 'led'**. If there is to be another revolution, it will perhaps be Clover, who has witnessed the whole process already, who will be instrumental in bringing it about. There is still a sense of hope left for the reader, especially if we remember that Orwell was a great champion of the working class, as is evident in his great work 'The Road to Wigan Pier'. He believed in a more equal society that, if the working class were active and involved, could be achieved. Clover, who is the **symbol** of the working classes in the novel, can instigate again that hope for a better life. However, this is only one interpretation, and there is a much bleaker reading of the novel as a story of inevitable shattered dreams. It seems unlikely that Clover, with her **'old, dim eyes'** can be a **symbol** of hope; she is physically frail and she, like the other animals, fails to challenge the pigs at any point in the novel. It seems that the negativity that Benjamin expresses is the underlying message of Animal Farm; Benjamin says that **'life would go on as it had always gone on- that is, badly.'** The donkey has no faith that society will ever change and his pessimism is, perhaps, our lasting message from the novel.

Essential Exam Tips

✓ Don't spend ages writing an introduction. Get stuck into the question straightaway.

✓ Keep an eye on the time. Write the time that you need to have finished this 'Animal Farm' question on a piece of paper and stick to it. If you run over too much, your response to the next question will suffer.

10 Setting
Exploration of the text

The story of 'Animal Farm' is set entirely within the boundaries of the farm, giving the story a simplicity and cohesion that enforces Orwell's messages. Yet the places in the novel are also rich in *symbolism* which adds to the reader's experience.

'on a sort of raised platform, Major was already ensconsed on his bed of straw'

- At the start of the novel, the animals gather in the barn to listen to Old Major's speech.
- The barn is the meeting place where the seeds of revolution are sown. The many details of the animals coming in creates a convincing and realistic setting: e.g. the horses stepping carefully and the pigeons flying to the rafters.
- Yet even as Old Major talks of equality, we wonder how this will play out as the pigs sit right at the front. Orwell uses *foreshadowing* to warn us that the pigs are dominant creatures on the farm.

Context: Orwell kept farm animals himself and used details from his observations to create the vivid world of Animal Farm.

'sweet summer grass... black earth... rich scent'

- The farm is a place of beauty and fertility. The sensory *adjectives* show the farm to be abundant and a place that can easily support the animals. This is evident in the **'black'** soil which is full of nutrients and the **'rich'** scent which promises fertility. It is a place worth having as it can be farmed for huge economic success.
- The animals initially want the farm to simply support themselves but the pigs' desire for power changes this; the farm is used to financially support the rulers and the oppressed workers are denied the products of their hard work.

Context: Orwell uses the farm as an *allegory* for Russia and the events of the early twentieth century. However, he sets the story on an English farm, perhaps to show his readers how the corruption of power can happen anywhere and to warn us to be vigilant and active in challenging our governments and leaders.

'unbelievable luxury... all were agreed that no animal must ever live there'

- The farm house is the comfortable stronghold of the humans.
- The animals are frightened of the farm house as it represents the tyranny of Jones. They are fascinated by the luxuries inside but are repelled by the corruption that this stands for.
- Later, the pigs take over the farm house as their living quarters, enjoying the same comforts as the humans and beginning to morph into their old masters. This change reflects the failure of the principles of Animalism.

Context: The farm house is the **allegorical symbol** for the Tsars' palaces, places of wealth and power in Russia under Romanov rule. The revolution was supposed to bring equality but Stalin and his ruling elite lived in great comfort while the ordinary people suffered.

'in glowing sentences, he painted a picture of Animal Farm... with electric light, hot and cold water'

- Snowball's ideas for the windmill are based on a desire for technology to improve the lives of the working animals.
- The windmill therefore becomes a structure which the animals work incredibly hard to build. They are inspired by the benefits it promises to their lives; the **adjective** '**glowing**' suggests Snowball's visionary hopes for the windmill as something bright and full of hope. Certainly, it seems to guarantee untold of luxuries which come with electricity and plumbing.
- Despite their enormous efforts, the animals see no benefits from the windmill. The pigs use the windmill for economic prosperity and use the wealth it brings purely for their own benefit.

Context: The windmill is the **allegorical symbol** for Stalin and his economic reforms. He changed Russia from an agrarian (farming) society to an industrialised one. The Russian workers toiled hard to achieve this but did not reap the benefits.

ANIMAL FARM — SETTING

'Foxwood... in a disgraceful condition... Pinchfield... cruelties that Frederick practised upon the animals'

- The neighbouring farms are neglected or are places of cruelty.
- Foxwood represents the capitalist West and Pinchfield is the symbolic place of Nazi Germany. Orwell shows the reader a world where tyranny and corruption exist everywhere.

Grade 9 Exploration:
Look at the text in a different way

How does the *structure* of the novel support Orwell's use of setting?

Orwell uses the careful **structure** of the novel along with the **symbolism** of the setting to strengthen the messages in his novel. The way the places are used and how they change as the story progresses heightens our understanding of the failure of the revolution.

An example is the knoll which is a small hill overlooking the farm. Just after the revolution, the animals visit it to view the place that they have miraculously acquired, seeing it as a place of beauty and wonder in the **'clear morning light'**. There is a sense of complete joy in the animals' behavior as they **'gambolled round and round, they hurled themselves into the air'**. The **dynamic verbs** of **'gambolled'** and **'hurled'** shows the animals' overwhelming excitement and show the hopeful enthusiasm with which they embrace their future. There is a sense of community here as the animals are described collectively, as one being with the pronoun **'they'** for all of the animals. This reflects the comraderie and equality which is the hallmark of their dream. Orwell **structures** the story to show how the revolution is failing by using the knoll again later in the novel when, after the bloodbath of the show trials and executions, the animals visit the knoll again but in a very different atmosphere. The farm is still beautiful and full of abundance as the sun **'gilded'** the fields with warm light but the animals' emotions are completely changed as **'the animals huddled about Clover, not speaking'**. The **verb 'huddled'** shows the animals' sense of fear and vulnerability and Clover dwells on how the farm is now a place where **'you had to watch your comrades torn to pieces'**. The **verb 'had'** shows how there is no autonomy for the ordinary animals within the dreadful violence of the farm. Orwell uses the sharp **contrast** between the earlier joy and freedom associated with the farm and the later misery and tyranny to reflect how the revolution fails.

A highly accomplished political writer, Orwell used the settings to work with the **structure** of the novel to reinforce one of his messages: that revolutions are almost always doomed to fail with one master replacing another. His own experiences fighting in the Spanish Civil War led to his cynicism about the effectiveness of revolutions.

Setting

The windmill is the *allegorical symbol* for Stalin's economic reforms. The rulers benefit from the changes but the workers do not reap the rewards of their labours.

'in glowing sentences, he painted a picture of Animal Farm... with electric light, hot and cold water'

The places in the novel have *symbolic* importance.

Orwell sets the story in England to show how corruption of power can happen anywhere.

'sweet summer grass... black earth... rich scent'

The farm is a place of fertility.

The places provide a realistic backdrop to the story.

'on a sort of raised platform, Major was already ensconced on his bed of straw'

The barn is where the seeds of rebellion are sown. The realistic details give the story an authenticity.

How does the novel's *structure* support the use of setting?

The knoll is used to contrast the animals' feelings of joy at the start with their despair after the executions.

The places remain the same but the atmosphere changes, documenting the failure of the revolution.

Sample GCSE Exam Question & Answer

Q: How does Orwell use setting in 'Animal Farm'?

✓ Start with the point that the farm provides a backdrop for the story

The story of 'Animal Farm' is set entirely within the boundaries of the farm, giving the story a simplicity and cohesion that enforces Orwell's messages. The reader experiences the narrative of the animals' hopes, revolution and eventual disillusionment firmly within the environment of the fields, orchards, hayfield and buildings of the farm that changes its name from Manor Farm to Animal Farm and back again. From the outset, Orwell gives the reader a convincing backdrop to his story as the animals gather in the barn to listen to Old Major's speech. There, '**on a sort of raised platform, Major was already ensconsed on his bed of straw**'. The barn is the meeting place where the seeds of revolution are sown. Orwell kept farm animals himself and used his own observations and experience in establishing a sense of place; the animals coming in creates a convincing and realistic setting and a sense of community is thus created. Yet even as Old Major talks of his dreams of equality, we wonder how this will play out as the pigs '**settled down in the straw immediately in front of the plaform**'. Orwell uses positioning within the setting to **foreshadow** how the pigs are natural leaders and are already asserting their dominance. Old Major's talk of equality is subtly undercut by this positioning.

✓ Move to the point that the settings help Orwell tell his *allegorical* story of Russia in the twentieth century

The meeting in the barn where the animals sing in solidarity and camaraderie is interrupted by shots fired by Jones from the farm house. The farm house is the comfortable stronghold of the humans and later, once Jones and his wife have fled, the animals are frightened of the farm house as it represents the tyranny of the humans. They are fascinated by the '**unbelievable luxury**' inside but are repelled by the corruption that this stands for, and '**all were agreed that no animal must ever live there**'. Yet it is not long before the pigs take over the farm house as their living quarters, enjoying the same comforts as the humans and, at the end, morphing into their old masters so that the pigs are indistinguishable from the humans. This change in the use of the farm house reflects the failure of the principles of Animalism, and also helps Orwell illustrate the events in Russia in the twentieth century. The farm house is the allegorical **symbol** for the Tsars' palaces, places of wealth and power in Russia under Romanov rule. The revolution was supposed to bring equality but Stalin and his ruling elite lived in luxury while the ordinary people suffered. The windmill is another place which Orwell uses to mirror events in Russia. Snowball's ideas for the windmill are based on a desire for technology to improve the lives of the working animals as '**in glowing sentences, he painted a picture of Animal Farm…with electric light, hot and cold water**'. The windmill therefore becomes a structure which the animals work incredibly hard to build. They are inspired by the benefits it promises to their lives; the **adjective 'glowing'** suggests Snowball's visionary hopes for the windmill as something bright and full of hope. Certainly, it seems to guarantee the luxuries which come with electricity and plumbing. Yet despite their enormous efforts, the animals see no benefits from the completed windmill as the pigs use it for economic prosperity and harnessing the wealth it brings purely for their own benefit. The windmill is the allegorical **symbol** for Stalin and his economic reforms. He changed Russia from an agrarian (farming) society to an industrialised one. The Russian workers toiled hard to achieve this but did not reap the benefits.

✓ Explore how Orwell uses setting and *structure* together to reinforce his message

Yet the settings are not just **allegorical symbols** for the Soviet Union. A highly accomplished political writer, Orwell used the settings to work with the **structure** of the novel to reinforce one of his messages: that revolutions are almost always doomed to fail with one master replacing another. His own experiences fighting

66   SETTING   ANIMAL FARM

in the Spanish Civil War led to his cynicism about the effectiveness of revolutions, and Orwell uses the careful **structure** of the novel along with the **symbolism** of the setting to strengthen this idea. The way the places are used and how they change as the story progresses heightens our understanding of the failure of the revolution. An example is the knoll which is a small hill overlooking the farm. Just after the revolution, the animals visit it to view the place that they have miraculously acquired, seeing it as a place of beauty and wonder in the **'clear morning light'**. There is a sense of complete joy in the animals' behavior as they **'gambolled round and round, they hurled themselves into the air'**. The **dynamic verbs** of **'gambolled'** and **'hurled'** reflect the animals' overwhelming excitement and show the hopeful enthusiasm with which they embrace their future. There is a sense of community here as the animals are described collectively, as one being with the **pronoun 'they'** for all of the animals. This reflects the comraderie and equality which is the hallmark of their dream. Interestingly, Orwell departs from his usual detached, unemotional narrative style in the sentence **'yes, it was theirs- everything that they could see was theirs!'** The **exclamatory sentence** reflects the wonder of the animals' achievement and the **repetition** of the **pronoun 'theirs'** shows how the animals have become their own masters, in control of the farm and their own lives. Orwell **structures** the story to show how the revolution is failing by using the knoll again later in the novel when, after the bloodbath of the show trials and executions, the animals visit the knoll again but in a very different atmosphere. The farm is still beautiful and full of abundance as the sun **'gilded'** the fields with warm light but the animals' emotions are completely changed as **'the animals huddled about Clover, not speaking'**. The **verb 'huddled'** shows the animals' sense of fear and vulnerability and Clover dwells on how the farm is now a place where **'you had to watch your comrades torn to pieces'**. The **verb 'had'** shows how there is no autonomy for the ordinary animals within the dreadful violence of the farm. Orwell uses the sharp **contrast** between the earlier joy and freedom associated with the farm and the knoll and the later misery and tyanny to reflect how the revolution fails.

> ✓ **Continue to make the point that the settings within the novel strengthen Orwell's messages**

The setting of the farm as a place of beauty is established several times throughout the novel and, even though the behaviour of the characters such as Napoleon deteriorates, the farm itself remains a constant place of fertility and lush richness. The sensory **adjectives** in the description of the farm with its **'sweet summer grass... black earth... rich scent'** show the farm to be abundant and a place that can easily support the animals. This is evident in the **'black'** soil which is full of nutrients and the **'rich'** scent which promises fertility. It is a place worth having as it can be farmed for huge economic success. The animals initially plan to use the farm to simply support themselves but the pigs' desire for power changes this; the farm is used to financially support the rulers and the workers are oppressed, denied the products of their hard work. Although Orwell uses the farm as an **allegory** for Russia and the events of the early twentieth century, he creates a setting of a farm which is in the heart of the English countryside. He did this, perhaps, to show his readerships how the corruption of power can happen anywhere and to warn his readers to be vigilant and active in challenging their governments and leaders. Certainly corruption is shown in the other settings of the novel with **'Foxwood... in a disgraceful condition... Pinchfield... cruelties that Frederick practised upon the animals'**. The neighbouring farms are neglected or places of cruelty. Foxwood represents the capitalist West and Pinchfield is the symbolic place of Nazi Germany, and Orwell shows the reader through his settings a world where tyranny and corruption exists everywhere. It is a sobering and poignant message.

11 Genre & Narrative
Exploration of the text

'Animal Farm' has sold millions of copies worldwide ever since its publication in 1945. This chapter explores how Orwell constructs an engaging, thought-provoking story.

'cruel whips no more shall crack'

- Old Major teaches the animals the 'Beasts of England' song; one of the lines is **'cruel whips no more shall crack'**.

- The opening of the novel gives us an insight into the harsh, miserable world of the animals and the reader sees the need for hopes and dreams in the face of Jones' mistreatment. We are firmly on the animals' side.

- Old Major is the figure of hope at the start of the novel. He inspires the animals to examine their miserable lives and imagine a future world where they can be free from slavery and enjoy equality.

- He is an eloquent orator and shows the power of language to ignite hope. Here, the lyrics paint a picture of a world free from **'cruel whips'** that **'crack'**. The hard c consonants capture the pain of the whips that the animals endure with the ***emotive language*** inspiring them to be free from their torture. Old Major's use of the ***modal verb* 'shall'** shows a strong level of certainty; he sees this future utopia as an event that will definitely happen and his certainty excites the animals and, in turn, the reader, that society might change.

Context: 'Animal Farm' is an *allegory* of Russia and the start of the novel mirrors the inspirational Karl Marx, who is represented by Old Major, setting out the ideas of communism. These ideas were later used by the Bolsheviks to encourage the Russian workers to rise up against the corrupt Romanov regime, just as the pigs take on Old Major's ideas to form Animalism.

> 'they gambolled round and round, they hurled themselves into the air'

- As the humans flee after the revolution, the animals experience great joy as their dream comes true, leaping and jumping round the farm that is now theirs. Orwell's narrative captures their ecstasy.
- The **dynamic verbs** of **'gambolled'** and **'hurled'** show the animals' overwhelming excitement and show the hopeful enthusiasm with which they embrace their future.
- There is a sense of community here as the animals are described collectively, as one being **'the animals'** and then with the **pronoun 'they'**. This reflects the camaraderie and equality which is the hallmark of their dream.

Context: Orwell originally called his novel 'Animal Farm; a fairy tale'. There is a sense of a fairy tale here with the talking, emotional animals and their extraordinary achievement.

> 'Smiling beatifically, and wearing both his decorations, Napoleon reposed... with the money at his side'

- Napoleon triumphantly displays the money he has received in payment for the timber. He is essentially greedy and ostentatious (a show-off) as he actually lies amongst the piles of bank notes.
- Orwell uses **satire** in the image of Napoleon **'smiling beatifically'**; the **adverb 'beatifically'** means saint-like but Napoleon is behaving in the exact opposite way, signalling to us that Orwell is making Napoleon a figure of fun.

Context: Joseph Stalin created a cult of personality that helped him maintain power through creating an impression of himself as god-like.

> 'in those days they were slaves and now they were free, and that made all the difference'

- Orwell uses **irony** when he relates the animals' justifications for their miserable lives which the revolution has not changed.
- The simplistic **tone** is created from the **monosyllabic words**, reflecting the animals' limited understanding of their situation. The irony is in that they are still slaves and not free at all and, far from **'all the difference'**, there is no difference at all in their situation.

ANIMAL FARM — GENRE & NARRATIVE

'But alas! His strength had left him'

- Boxer tries to kick his way out of the horse slaughterer's van but is too weak.
- There is a strong sense of **pathos** in the once-strong Boxer left too weak to save himself. There is **irony** in that he has worn himself out in the cause of the revolution yet at the end the revolution completely fails him.
- The author's voice clearly directs our response to sympathy in the phrase **'but alas!'** The **exclamatory phrase** openly grieves for Boxer's inability to escape his fate and captures the tragedy that is Boxer's horrid, brutal death. It is a marked change from the usual dispassionate, factual narration that tells most of the story and so highlights the importance of the incident.

Grade 9 Exploration:
Look at the text in a different way

Which genre does 'Animal Farm' best fit into?

Fairy tale: A story of talking animals and the overthrow of the evil regime of Mr Jones are the fundamentals of the classic fairy-tale. Yet Orwell subverts this genre as the evil is not ultimately defeated and, indeed, returns in full force as Napoleon walks on two trotters clutching a whip. Orwell's original manuscript titled the story 'Animal Farm: a fairy tale' yet this subheading was dropped by some publishers.

Beast fable: Orwell drew on the literary tradition of the beast fable, made famous by Aesop. This genre tells a story about human behaviour but uses animals as the characters. There is a moral to be learned. Orwell's moral or lesson that we should take from 'Animal Farm' is that humankind is flawed by a desire for power which corrupts.

Satire: 'Animal Farm' can be read as a satire of how leaders take and hold onto power. Orwell was a political writer; he wrote other books which also tackled political issues such as '1984' which again shows the reader the dangers of totalitarian government.

Allegory: An allegory is a story with two meanings. 'Animal Farm' can be read as an **allegory** of Russia in the first half of the twentieth century. Orwell was horrified at events in Russia and used 'Animal Farm' to illustrate what had happened to the country after the 1917 revolution.

Reader response criticism is a literary theory which focuses on what an individual reader brings to a text based on their own experiences and circumstance. How a reader responds to 'Animal Farm' depends on many factors. So, for example, Orwell received letters from intellectual colleagues and friends who had thoroughly enjoyed the novel for its powerful messages about corruption but whose young children had also read it and loved it on a much simpler level. This shows the universal appeal of the story and reflects Orwell's mastery as a novelist.

Genre & Narrative

Old Major has a vision of a better, happier society that ensures the story begins on a promising, fairy-tale style note.

'cruel whips no more shall crack'

The story opens with inspirational hope.

The simplistic **tone** is created from the **monosyllabic words**, reflecting the animals' limited understanding of their situation.

'in those days they were slaves and now they were free, and that made all the difference'

Orwell uses irony to show how the revolution fails.

Boxer's death highlights the lesson that power corrupts.

'But alas! His strength failed'

The **exclamatory phrase** directs our response to pity Boxer and his dreadful death. It also shows us how corrupt the pigs have become.

Which genre does 'Animal Farm' fit into?

Fairy tale and/or beast fable

Allegory and/or political satire

ANIMAL FARM GENRE & NARRATIVE 71

Sample GCSE Exam Question & Answer

Q: How far should 'Animal Farm' be read as a political or historical piece of writing?

✓ Start with the point that 'Animal Farm' can be read as a historical account

'Animal Farm' has sold millions of copies worldwide ever since its publication in 1945 and there is no doubt that Orwell constructed an engaging, thought-provoking story. Yet the genre of the story is not nailed down and it is possible to read the story of the downtrodden animals rebelling in a number of ways. Certainly, one of these ways is that the story is an **allegory** of the Russian historical events of the first part of the twentieth century. The **chronological structure** of the novel faithfully follows the events that happened in the Soviet Union, and this is evident from the opening when Old Major inspires the animals to examine their miserable lives and imagine a future world where they can be free from slavery and enjoy equality. This mirrors the inspirational Karl Marx, who is represented by Old Major, setting out the ideas of communism which later were used by the revolutionaries to encourage the Russian workers to rise up against the corrupt Romanov regime. Old Major teaches the animals the 'Beasts of England' song; one of the lines is **'cruel whips no more shall crack'** and in this line the reader is given an insight into the harsh, miserable world of the animals who suffer from Jones' mistreatment. Old Major is an eloquent orator and shows the power of language to ignite hope. Here, the lyrics paint a picture of a world free from **'cruel whips'** that **'crack'**, the hard c consonants capturing the pain of the whips that the animals endure and the **emotive language** inspiring them to be free from their torture. Old Major's use of the **modal verb 'shall'** shows a strong level of certainty; he sees this future utopia as an event that will definitely happen and his certainty excites the animals and, in turn, the reader, that society might change. This inspiration mirrors Karl Marx's Communist Manifesto which was used by the Russian revolutionaries in the early twentieth century. The rest of 'Animal Farm' tracks the historical events; for example, the animals' revolution is the 1917 revolution in Russia, and the Battle of the Cowshed shows the attempts of the anti-communists to fight back against the Bolsheviks.

✓ Move to the point that the story can be read as a political satire

While the events in the novel do allow the reader to learn much about the history of the Soviet Union, it is perhaps as a political satire that 'Animal Farm' is famous for. Orwell was a political writer whose work often explored ideas about society and power; his novel '1984 'is set in a dystopian world of government control. 'Animal Farm' also fits into this genre of a fictional world where the characters are controlled by their leaders, and Orwell uses **irony** to show us how power will corrupt. We see this in his depiction of the leaders, who are pigs. This is itself is witty, and Orwell constantly presents Napoleon with an ironic edge. For example, Napoleon triumphantly displays the money he has received in payment for the timber: **'smiling beatifically, and wearing both his decorations, Napoleon reposed...with the money at his side'**. Orwell uses **satire** to undermine Napoleon in the image of Napoleon **'smiling beatifically'**; the **adverb** **'beatifically'** means saint-like but Napoleon is behaving in the exact opposite way, signalling to us that Orwell is making Napoleon a figure of fun. This is reinforced later when we find out that the bank notes are fakes. Orwell shows us that even if a leader has complete power, it does not mean that we should respect him or her. Another example of Orwell's use of **satire** is when he relates the animals' justifications for their miserable lives which the revolution has not changed: the animals tell themselves that in Jones' **'days they were slaves and now they were free, and that made all the difference'**. The simplistic **tone** is created from the **monosyllabic words**, reflecting the animals' limited understanding of their situation. The **irony** is in that they are still slaves and not free at all and, far from **'all the difference'**, there is no difference at all in their situation. Orwell is certainly warning us that we need to be active and vigilant against our leaders through his novel and as such it is most certainly a political work.

☑ Make the point that the story can also be read in other ways

Yet it does not have to be read as political work; indeed, Orwell's original manuscript titled the story 'Animal Farm: a fairy tale' yet this subheading was dropped by some publishers. A story of talking animals and the overthrow of the evil regime of Mr Jones are the fundamentals of the classic fairy-tale. We see this fairy tale style in the successful revolution. As the humans flee after the revolution, the animals experience great joy as their dream comes true, leaping and jumping round the farm that is now theirs. Orwell's narrative captures their ecstasy in the sentences **'they gambolled round and round, they hurled themselves into the air'**. The **dynamic verbs** of **'gambolled'** and **'hurled'** show the animals' overwhelming excitement and show the hopeful enthusiasm with which they embrace their future. We see a real sense of community here as the animals are described collectively, as one being- the animals. This reflects the camaraderie and equality which is the hallmark of their dream. There is a sense of a fairy tale here with the talking, emotional animals and their extraordinary achievement. Yet the euphoria of the animals is short-lived and Orwell subverts this genre as the evil is not ultimately defeated and, indeed, returns in full force as Napoleon walks on two trotters clutching a whip.

☑ Consider whether the novel best fits the genre of beast fable

This negative ending certainly suggests that the novel is a beast fable. The talking animals who have human emotions and personalities is a hallmark of the beast fable, made famous by Aesop's fables. There is a moral to be learned from these fables and Orwell's moral or lesson that we should take from 'Animal Farm' is that humankind is flawed by a desire for power which corrupts. This lesson is taught to us throughout the novel, perhaps most painfully when Boxer tries to kick his way out of the horse slaughterer's van but is too weak. There is a strong sense of **pathos** in the once-strong Boxer left too weak to save himself and **irony** in that he has worn himself out in the cause of the revolution yet at the end the revolution completely fails him. The author's voice clearly directs our response to sympathy in the phrase **'But alas! His strength had left him'**. The **exclamatory phrase** openly grieves for Boxer's inability to escape his fate and captures the tragedy that is Boxer's horrid, brutal death. It is a marked change from the usual dispassionate, factual narration that tells most of the story and so highlights the importance of the incident. This incident **structurally** marks another point for the reader in the catalogue of the failure of equality. Boxer's faith in the revolution and his plans for retirement are shown to be worthless; the revolution has no use for workers who cannot work and so dispenses of them in a ruthless fashion. Reader response criticism is a literary theory which focuses on what an individual reader brings to a text based on their own experiences and circumstance. How a reader responds to 'Animal Farm' depends on many factors. So, for example, Orwell received letters from intellectual colleagues and friends who had thoroughly enjoyed the novel for its powerful messages about corruption but whose young children had also read it and loved it on a much simpler level. This shows the universal appeal of the story and reflects Orwell's mastery as a novelist. While we can certainly read 'Animal Farm' as a political satire, it can be enjoyed on many other levels.

Essential Exam Tips

☑ Don't worry about writing a long conclusion. It isn't necessary.

☑ Aim for four detailed paragraphs; your response will be evaluated on quality not quantity but it's difficult to make your response good if it is brief or lacking in detail.

12 Failure of the Revolution
Exploration of a theme

Orwell uses 'Animal Farm' to show the failure of the animals' revolution that was supposed to bring equality. The story gives us a wider message: that revolutions will always fail if there are power-hungry leaders who have no interest in equality and these leaders are not challenged.

'All animals are equal'

- Old Major's speech establishes the fundamental principle of Animalism.
- It is an ideal that seems achievable and which inspires the animals who live miserable lives that are completely under the control of the farmer.
- Yet already, there is a sense of fanaticism and power in the wording of the commandment. The **declarative sentence** is forceful and the other commandments are similar or use the **modal verb 'shall'** which seems to imply that the pigs are imposing his will on the intellectually weaker animals. The pigs appear fanatical in their belief in Animalism, for example refusing to allow Mollie to wear the ribbons that she loves. Mollie's wishes are not listened to, making us see how hard it is for equality to be achieved.

'Never mind the milk, comrades' cried Napoleon, placing himself in front of the buckets'

- The pigs take control of the milk which the reader later learns has been mixed into the pigs' mash. Even though the revolution is only hours old, the pigs take the first opportunity to benefit from the overthrow of the humans.
- Orwell meant this incident to be a turning point in the novel, showing through the **structure** of the novel how the dream of the revolution is doomed even as it is beginning because of the self-interest of the pigs. Their natural intelligence and cunning mean that they have no intention of all the animals being equal and they take advantage of the other animals.

Context: Napoleon is the *allegorical* figure for Stalin, the dictator who used the revolution to take complete control of Russia. Just as Stalin manipulated the revolution, so does Napoleon, showing how the dream of equality is eroded.

'nine enormous dogs wearing brass-studded collars...dashed straight for Snowball'

- Napoleon uses the dogs as a way controlling the animals. Here, he uses them to get rid of his rival, Snowball.

- The **adjectives** '**enormous**' and '**brass-studded**' in the description help create a sense of violent brutality while the **verb** '**dashed**' shows their speed. Napoleon has the dogs well-trained in his service and uses them ruthlessly to crush any opposition.

- One of the fundamental cornerstones of an equal society is free speech and here the reader sees how Napoleon dismisses this concept and seizes control.

- Throughout the novel, Napoleon uses the dogs to stamp out opposition and impose his totalitarian rule, showing he has no interest in equality.

Context: The dogs are the allegorical representation of Stalin's brutal secret police, the NKVD.

'No animal shall drink alcohol to excess'

- It is Squealer who changes the fifth commandment on the wall, showing how far the principles of Animalism have been eroded and how swiftly the revolution is failing.

- Orwell uses **satire** here as Squealer changes this particular commandment while drunk, ensuring that we condemn the hypocrisy of the pigs.

- The commandments are changed throughout the story; the power of the written word is in the hands of the educated pigs, not in the hands of the animals who struggle to read.

Context: Stalin used written propaganda to control the population through the government-controlled newspaper Pravda. In the **allegorical** tale of 'Animal Farm', the written commandments and the way they are altered show how the semi-literate animals are controlled by written language.

'it was impossible to say which was which'

- At the end of the novel, Napoleon is walking on two legs, sleeping in a bed and is, essentially, a human; so much so that the watching animals cannot tell Napoleon and Mr Pilkington apart.
- Napoleon's transformation into a human reflects the **cyclical structure** of the novel and shows us that the failure of the revolution was a foregone conclusion. The animals are in an even worse position than they were at the beginning of the story; far from a position of equality, they are in a position of complete subjugation.

Context: Orwell intended his novel to show how revolutions were almost inevitably doomed to fail with one master being exchanged for another. Orwell had actively participated in the Spanish Civil War and had become cynical of revolutions and those who lead them.

Grade 9 Exploration:
Look at the theme in a different way

Was the failure of the revolution for equality inevitable?

Yes: Orwell shows us through the **cyclical structure** of the novel that the failure of the revolution was inevitable, perhaps because of human nature. Napoleon's greed for power is a human trait which always leads to an unequal society. Similarly, the different abilities of people show how hard it is for equality to be achieved; the pigs' natural intelligence gives them a huge advantage over the other animals, reflecting a society which is inherently unequal.

No: At the end, Clover is, perhaps, a **symbol** of hope. The **cyclical structure** of the novel with the pigs and humans morphing into one means that the reader wonders whether there will be another revolution, and certainly Clover is not so downtrodden that she cannot investigate what the pigs are up to. The animals creep up to the farmhouse and **'paused, half-frightened to go on, but Clover led the way in.'** The **conjunction** 'but' emphasises the courage of the old horse and her authority is clear in the **verb 'led'**. If there is to be another revolution, it will perhaps be Clover, who has witnessed the whole process already, who will be instrumental in bringing it about. Next time, the animals might have learned their lessons and be able to successfully create a society which is more equal.

Orwell was a great champion of the working class, as depicted in his great work 'The Road to Wigan Pier'. He believed in a more equal society that, if the working class were active and involved, could be achieved. Clover, who is the **symbol** of the working classes in the novel, can instigate again that hope for a better life in a fairer society.

Old Major inspires the animals to rebel against their master who keeps them in a condition of miserable slavery.

Napoleon takes the first opportunity to benefit from the revolution by taking the milk, undermining the fine talk of equality for all.

'all animals are equal'

'Never mind the milk, comrades!'

The revolution is based on a desire for equality.

The revolution begins to fail on the first day.

Failure of the revolution

The revolution completely fails.

Is Orwell giving us a message that equality is unachievable and revolutions will always fail?

'it was impossible to say which was which'

Yes: The *cyclical structure* of the novel shows us that the failure of the revolution was inevitable.

At the end, the pigs are as corrupt and cruel as the humans, with the other animals in a position of subjugation.

No: The *cyclical structure* of the novel shows how another revolution is possible and this time it might achieve the aim of a more equal society.

Sample GCSE Exam Question & Answer

Q: 'The animals' revolution was intended to bring about a fair and equal society yet it ultimately failed.'
Write about how Orwell presents the failure of the revolution for equality.

✓ **Start with the point that the principle of equality is crucial to the revolution**

Orwell uses 'Animal Farm' to show the failure of the animals' revolution that was supposed to bring equality. The story gives us a wider message: that revolutions will always fail if there are power-hungry leaders who have no interest in equality and if these leaders are not challenged. Yet, at the start of the novel, the animals are inspired by the prospect of equality. Old Major's speech in Chapter One establishes the fundamental principle of Animalism, that **'all animals are equal'**. It is an ideal that seems achievable and which inspires the animals who live miserable lives, completely under the control of the farmer. Yet already, there is, perhaps, a sense of fanaticism and power in the wording of the commandment. The **declarative sentence** is forceful and the other commandments are similar or use the **modal verb** **'shall'** which seems to imply that the pig is imposing his will on the intellectually weaker animals. Later, the pigs appear fanatical in their belief in Animalism, for example refusing to allow Mollie to wear the ribbons that she loves. Mollie's wishes are not listened to, making us see how hard it is for equality to be achieved.

✓ **Move to the point that ideas of equality are quickly challenged and the revolution begins to fail**

This is borne out through subsequent events. The revolution comes with all its ecstacy and hope for equality yet almost immediately begins to falter. Even though the revolution is only hours old, the pigs take the first opportunity to benefit from the overthrow of the humans. The pigs take control of the milk which the reader later learns has been mixed into the pigs' mash; Napoleon cries **'never mind the milk, comrades'** and places himself in front of the buckets. Orwell meant this incident to be a turning point in the novel, showing through the **structure** of the novel how the dream of the revolution is doomed even as it is beginning because of the self-interest of the pigs. Their natural intelligence and cunning mean that they have no intention of all the animals being equal and they take advantage of the other animals. Already the reader is uneasily aware that the prospect of true equality is undermined. There is **irony** in the way that Napoleon addresses the other animals with the title **'comrades'** which implies complete solidarity and commitment even as he plans to betray them. Napoleon is the allegorical figure for Stalin, the brutal dictator who used the revolution to take complete control of Russia. Just as Stalin manipulated the revolution, so does Napoleon, showing how the dream of equality is quickly eroded.

✓ **Move to the point that the principles of equality are constantly eroded as the revolution continues to fail**

As the months pass, the revolution continues to falter, with the novel chronicling how the dream of equality is chipped away by Napoleon and his elite pigs. Napoleon uses the dogs as a way of controlling the animals, getting rid of his opposition with **'nine enormous dogs wearing brass-studded collars** (who) **dashed straight for Snowball'**. The **adjectives** **'enormous'** and **'brass-studded'** in the description help create a sense of violent brutality while the **verb** **'dashed'** shows their speed. Napoleon has the dogs well-trained in his service and uses them ruthlessly to crush any opposition. One of the fundamental cornerstones of an equal society is free speech and here the reader sees how Napoleon dismisses this concept and seizes control. Throughout the novel, Napoleon uses the dogs to stamp out opposition and impose his totalitarian rule, showing he has no interest in equality, just as Stalin crushed dissent and smothered equality with his NKVD secret police. Intimidation and terror tactics are proven ways to ensure an inherently unequal society.

☑ Explore whether Orwell's message is that equality is impossible and that revolutions are pointless

Orwell shows us through the **cyclical structure** of the novel that the failure of the revolution was always inevitable, perhaps because of human nature. Napoleon's greed for power is a human trait which always leads to an unequal society. Similarly, the different abilities of people show how hard it is for equality to be achieved; the pigs' natural intelligence gives them a huge advantage over the other animals, reflecting a society which is inherently unequal. Yet this pessimistic message is not necessarily the only message that Orwell gives us. Orwell was a democratic socialist and as such was a great champion of the working class, as depicted in his great work 'The Road to Wigan Pier'. He believed in a more equal society that, if the working class were active and involved, could be achieved. He uses the character of Clover, who is the **symbol** of the working classes in the novel, to instigate again that hope for a better life in a fairer society. The **cyclical structure** of the novel with the pigs and humans morphing into one means that the reader wonders whether there will be another, more successful revolution. Clover is not so downtrodden that she cannot investigate what the pigs are up to. The animals creep up to the farmhouse and **'paused, half-frightened to go on, but Clover led the way in.'** The **conjunction 'but'** emphasises the courage of the old horse and her authority is clear in the **verb 'led'**. If there is to be another revolution, it will perhaps be Clover, who has witnessed the whole process already and seen its pitfalls, who will be instrumental in bringing it about. Next time, the animals might have learned their lessons and stage a revolution that does successfully create a society which is more equal.

📝 Essential Exam Tips

- ☑ Re-read the novel a fortnight before the exam from start to finish. It should only take a few hours to do this.

- ☑ Start revising for the exams early. Revising in ten minute bursts from the end of Year 10 can make a huge difference and reduces the last minute panic before your exams.

Quotations
Recap & Revise

Chapter One

'on a sort of raised platform, Major was already ensconsed on his bed of straw'
Old Major sits at the front to tell the animals about his dream.

'Old Major... majestic-looking pig... wise and benevolent'
Old Major is described in a positive way.

'pigs... settled down in the straw immediately in front of the platform'
The pigs sit at the front during the meeting in the barn.

'Remove man from the scene, and the root cause of hunger and overwork is abolished forever'
Old Major explains to the animals how they are exploited by the humans.

'cut your throat and boil you down'
Old Major tells Boxer what will happen to him when he is old and weak.

'All animals are equal'
Old Major tells the animals that they are equal and the pigs use this as the central principle of Animalism.

'cruel whips no more shall crack'
Old Major sings of a future world free from pain and torture.

Chapter Two

'Napoleon...large, rather fierce-looking Berkshire boar'
Napoleon is described as a powerful pig.

'not much of a talker'
Napoleon is quiet but powerful.

'brilliant talker...he had a way of skipping from side to side and whisking his tail which was very persuasive'
Squealer is highly articulate.

'the others said... he could turn black into white'
Squealer is expert at twisting the truth.

'Sugarcandy Mountain'
Moses the raven tells the animals about a wonderful afterlife.

'they gambolled round and round, they hurled themselves into the air'
The animals are overjoyed at the success of the revolution.

'sweet summer grass... black earth... rich scent'
The farm is a place of fertility.

'unbelievable luxury... all were agreed that no animal must ever live there'
The animals are impressed but repelled by the farm house.

'Never mind the milk, comrades!' cried Napoleon, placing himself in front of the buckets'
Napoleon takes the milk for the pigs' own use.

Chapter Three

'did not actually work but directed and supervised the others... 'Gee up, comrade'!'

The pigs take the roles of leaders.

'I will work harder'
Boxer is a strong, determined worker.

'indefatigable'
Snowball is incredibly energetic in organising his committees.

'almost every animal on the farm was literate in some degree'
Snowball succeeds in teaching the animals to read and write.

'could not get beyond the letter D'
Boxer struggles to learn to read.

'Mollie refused to learn any but the five letters which spelt out her own name'
Mollie is not interested in reading.

'nine puppies... Napoleon... (said) that he would make himself responsible for their education'
Napoleon takes the nine puppies away to be educated by himself.

'it is for *your* sake that we drink that milk and eat those apples'
Squealer convinces the animals that the pigs take the milk for selfless purposes.

'Surely there is no one among you who wants to see Jones come back?'
Squealer uses the language of fear to persuade the animals to accept the pigs' decisions.

Chapter Four

'Foxwood... in a disgraceful condition'
Pilkington neglects his farm.

'without halting for an instant'
Snowball bravely leads the animals during the Battle of the Cowshed.

'great iron-shod hoofs'
Boxer has enormous physical strength.

Chapter Five

'Life would go on as it had always gone on - that is, badly'
Benjamin shows a pessimistic view of life.

'in glowing sentences he painted a picture of Animal Farm... with electric light, hot and cold water'
Snowball tells the animals how the windmill will improve their lives.

'nine enormous dogs wearing brass-studded collars...dashed straight for Snowball'
Napoleon uses the dogs to terrorise Snowball into leaving the farm.

'Napoleon is always right'
Boxer takes this sentence as a motto.

'Squealer spoke so persuasively, and the three dogs who happened to be with him growled so threateningly'
Squealer and the dogs are used to control the animals.

Chapter Seven

'He stole the corn, he upset the milk-pails, he broke the eggs'
The exiled Snowball is used as a scapegoat for everything that goes wrong.

'animals huddled about Clover'
The animals look to Clover for comfort after the executions.

'As Clover looked down the hillside her eyes filled with tears'
Clover is deeply upset by the show trials and executions.

'you had to watch your comrades torn to pieces'
Clover reflects on the horrors of the executions.

'if she could have spoken her thoughts'
Clover struggles to articulate her thoughts.

Chapter Eight

'Pinchfield... cruelties that Frederick practised upon the animals'
Frederick's farm is a place of pain and misery.

'Smiling beatifically, and wearing both his decorations, Napoleon reposed... with the money at his side'
Napoleon shows off the money from the timber to the animals.

'Squealer, who had unaccountably been absent'
Squealer hides while the animals are defending the farm.

'No animal shall drink alcohol to excess'
The pigs change the commandment to suit their new habit of drinking alcohol.

Chapter Nine

'in those days they were slaves and now they were free, and that made all the difference'
The animals tell themselves that their lives are better.

'Fools! Fools! Do you not see what is written on the side of that van?'
Benjamin reads the sign on the horse slaughterer's van.

'But alas! His strength had left him'
Boxer is too weak to escape from the horse slaughterer's cart.

Chapter Ten

'four legs good, two legs *better*!'
The sheep's chant silences the other animals and shows how the revolution has completely failed.

'paused, half-frightened to go on, but Clover led the way in'
Clover leads the animals to the farm house.

'old, dim eyes'
Clover struggles to see the pigs and humans.

'it was impossible to say which was which'
The pigs look the same as the humans.

Glossary
Explanation of terms

ADJECTIVE - a word that describes a noun **e.g. 'large boar'**

ADVERB - a word that describes a verb **e.g. 'smiling beatifically'**

ALLITERATION - repetition of the same letter in words next to or near each other **e.g. 'cruel whips...crack'**

CHRONOLOGICAL STRUCTURE - when a novel is structured in time order

CLAUSE - a group of words that contains a verb

COLLOQUIAL - every day words and phrases

CONDITIONAL TENSE - tense that speculates on what might or could happen **e.g. 'if she could have spoken her thoughts'**

CONJUNCTION - word that joins two clauses **e.g. '... paused, half-frightened to go on, but Clover led the way in'**

CONTRAST/JUXTAPOSITION - use of opposites **e.g. Mr Jones' drunken cruel leadership contrasts with Old Major's dignified talk of equality**

CYCLICAL STRUCTURE - when the ending of a story links back to the beginning with the same events happening

DECLARATIVE SENTENCE - a sentence that states a fact **e.g. 'All animals are equal'**

DETERMINER - words used to modify a noun **e.g. 'in some degree'**

DIALOGUE - conversation between characters

DYNAMIC VERB - verb that shows an action **e.g. 'they gambolled round and round'**

EMOTIVE LANGUAGE - language that evokes emotion in the reader

EXCLAMATORY PHRASE OR SENTENCE - a sentence or phrase that shows excitement or emotion **e.g. 'But alas!'**

FORESHADOWING - to give a warning of a future event **e.g. the pigs' positioning at the front of the barn during Major's speech foreshadows how they will take control**

IMAGE - powerful words or phrase that paints a picture in our heads

IMPERATIVE VERBS - verbs that give orders e.g. **'Gee up!'**

INTENSIFIER - word that strengthens an adverb or adjective **e.g. 'so persuasively'**

IRONY - using language to show the opposite of what is stated **e.g. 'in those days they were slaves and now they were free, and that made all the difference'**

JUXTAPOSITION - see contrast

LIST - a group of ordered items or actions **e.g. 'He stole the corn, he upset the milk-pails, he broke the eggs'**

METAPHOR - descibing a person or object as something else **e.g. 'Snowball... painted a picture'**

MINOR SENTENCE - an incomplete sentence **e.g. 'Fools!'**

MODAL VERBS - verbs that show a level of certainty **e.g. 'I will work harder'**

ANIMAL FARM **GLOSSARY**

MONOSYLLABIC WORDS -words with one syllable **e.g. 'cut your throat'**

NOUN - name of an object/place/time/emotion

OMNISCIENT NARRATOR - narrator who can tell the feelings and thoughts of characters because the narrator is not part of the story

PATHOS - sadness

PLOT DEVICE - technique used to move narrative along

PRONOUN - a word that replaces a proper noun **e.g. ' it is for <u>your</u> sake that we drink that milk and eat those apples'**

RHETORICAL QUESTION - question that does not need an answer **e.g. 'Surely there is no one among you who wants to see Jones come back?**

REPETITION - when a word or phrase is repeated e.g. **'<u>so</u> persuasively... <u>so</u> threateningly'**

SETTING - where a scene is played out **e.g. the opening setting is in the barn**

SIMILE - describing a person or object as something else using 'like' or 'as' e.g.

SATIRE - the use of humour or irony to criticise a person or a viewpoint

STRUCTURE - the order in which events happen in a story

SYMBOL - when an object/person stands for something else **e.g Clover is a symbol of hope**

SYNTAX - order of words in a sentence

THIRD PERSON NARRATIVE - story told using 'he' 'they' etc. The narrator is not part of the story.

TONE - mood or atmosphere

VERB - an action word **e.g. 'but Clover <u>led</u> the way in'**

Lightning Source UK Ltd.
Milton Keynes UK
UKHW050610280622
405041UK00003B/65